The Call of God

Delegates from El Agustino attending the third National
Meeting of Communal Banks in the Peruvian city of Huancayo

The Call of God

Women Doing Theology in Peru

Tom Powers, S.J.

State University of New York Press

Photos courtesy of the author and Ofelia Montes López, Executive Director, SEA, Lima.

Published by
State University of New York Press, Albany

Printed in the United States of America

For information, address State University of New York Press,
90 State Street, Suite 700, Albany, NY 12207

Production by Judith Block
Marketing by Jennifer Giovani

Library of Congress Cataloging-in-Publication Data

Powers, S.J., Tom
The call of God : women doing theology in Peru / Tom Powers.
p. cm.
Includes bibliographical references (p.) and index.
ISBN 0-7914-5789-3 (alk. paper) — ISBN 0-7914-5790-7 (pbk. : alk. paper)
1. Women in church work—Catholic Church. 2. Women in church work—Peru—Lima. 3. Servicios Educativos El Augustino. 4. Theology—Peru—Lima. I. title.

BX1485.L52 P68 2003
230'.082'0985—dc21

2002030449

10 9 8 7 6 5 4 3 2 1

Contents

Preface

In 1997 I arrived in Peru on an all-night flight from California. By six o'clock that morning, I was at one of the Jesuit residences in Lima, tired, trying to think in Spanish, and ready for some sleep. My Peruvian friend, Lucho Herrera, S.J., introduced me to a woman who was in the lobby of the residence. Her name was Ofelia Montes López and he said, "You must get to know her. She can teach you a lot." Little did I know how true his words were.

Sra. Montes López is the director of *Servicios Educativos El Agustino* (Educational Services El Agustino or SEA). SEA is the social outreach organization of the Jesuit parish in El Agustino, one of the poorest neighborhoods in Lima. As I grew to know Sra. Montes López and the women with whom she works at SEA, not only did I learn a great deal but I also found myself challenged, inspired, and lifted up by their faith, love, and dedication.

This book is about these women and the theology that emerges from their work and faith. It does not fall into any precise theological category—systematics, foundational, historical, or theological ethics—but is primarily a consideration of their volatile environment and the way in which they respond to it. I have focused on the women of El Agustino because I am interested in what women are doing theologically in the country that was the birthplace of liberation theology.

Almost half of the population of Peru has moved from the countryside to the cities in the past three decades. Thus, the women of SEA are a fair representation of the cultures, languages, and religious traditions found throughout Peru. Of course the poverty the people were fleeing has only grown worse and liberation can appear to be more removed than it was thirty years ago.

An inspiration for this book comes from the *Documents of the Thirty-fourth General Congregation of the Society of Jesus*' Decree 14, "Jesuits and the Situation of Women in Church and Civil Society." The decree invites "all Jesuits to listen carefully and courageously to the experience of women. . . . There is no substitute for such listening. More than anything else it will bring about change." The document goes on to state that

> unless we listen, any action we may take in this area, no matter how well intentioned, is likely to bypass the real concerns of women and to confirm male condescension and reinforce male dominance. Listening, in a spirit of partnership and equality, is the most practical response we can make and is the foundation for our mutual partnership to reform unjust structures.

The "call of God" is a phrase I heard repeatedly from the women of SEA. Much of what they do finds its origins in answering this call. What is meant, however, by "doing theology"? My starting point is the classical definition of theology as "faith seeking understanding." The faith of the women of El Agustino is obvious at first encounter. As one grows to know these women, it is also obvious that they think in ways that are rooted in the struggles and successes of their work with the poor. They may not use the terminology of trained theologians but they produce inspiring, action-provoking, Gospel-rooted results. They are experts at interpreting and responding to the signs of the times.

I worked with the women of El Agustino for one year and conducted numerous formal interviews and carried on innumerable informal conversations. As a white North American male and Jesuit priest, I tried to be sensitive to many dynamics: the propriety of relations between men and women in Peruvian society; what was and was not considered an appropriate question from a man; careful consideration of what was said and what was left unsaid; interaction with a priest in a highly clerical, culturally Catholic country; and being white in an environment where those of European ancestry have oppressed the poor for centuries.

Chapters 1–2 introduce the setting and context of Peru, Lima, and El Agustino, and the social, political, and church environments. Understanding the women of El Agustino requires an awareness of what they bring from the past and what they face in the present. Chapter 3 looks more personally at them: What is the foundation for their work? How do they sustain hope for themselves and become bearers of hope for others? How do they explore the mystery of God? What is their vision for the future?

Chapter 4 examines how suffering becomes a starting point for theological reflection and concrete accomplishments. In the promotion of life, the women discover how to answer the call of God. They embrace and challenge the institutional church, reflect on Scripture, and create life-changing organizations, all the time saving lives, lessening despair, and lifting up the possibility of creating lives of dignity and justice. This chapter seeks to explicate how they creatively and faithfully engage in doing theology. Chapter 5 suggests some future paths as the women continue to engage passionately with a rapidly changing world.

My thanks go out to the Jesuits in Peru for their unflagging support, in particular Lucho Herrera; Kevin Flaherty; Jaime O'Leary; Gerardo Aste; and Francisco Chamberlain; to the communities of Nuestra Señora de Fátima, Juniorado, and El Agustino; to Carlos Cardó Franco and Ernesto Cavassa, past and present provincials; to Fr. Gustavo Gutiérrez, OP for his time, patience, and wisdom; to Hal Sanks, S.J., for challenging and supporting me these many years; to Ada María Isasi-Díaz, who answered an e-mail and became a dear friend; to Alex García-Rivera for incisive insights; to Kap Stann and John Burnes for their astute comments; to Rita Stukey, IHM, and Amy Molina for their able assistance; to Nancy Ellegate at the State University of New York Press for believing in this book; and to all of the people who gave me their time and wisdom in the interviews.

And finally, this book is dedicated to the remarkable women of *Servicios Educativos El Agustino*. They are, indeed, "the best of liberation theologians." They would welcome your inquiries and can be reached at:

Servicios Educativos El Agustino (SEA)
Renán Olivera 249–El Agustino
Apartado 11-0038
Lima 10, Peru

Tel: 51 1 327-0784
Fax: 51 1 327-0175
E-mail: *SEA@amauta.rcp.net.pe*

Women community leaders of El Agustino

CHAPTER 1

Introduction

> *Women are filled with love and faith and give a lot to others. Their faith does not exist just in church but in their homes, the streets, and their places of work. Christ preached many things; things like loving others and sharing with the example of the multiplication of the loaves and fishes. And that is just what the women here do—in the* comedores *(communal dining rooms), the education projects, the communal banks. They multiply what isn't enough. And suddenly they do more than just practice a religion. They are doing what Christ said to do. They do it with much love and they confront problems just like Christ. And they pick up the whip when people take advantage of others; when there's injustice.*
>
> Rosa Castillo Reyes
> President
> *Club de Madres*
> (Mothers' Club)

This book aims to illuminate the words and deeds, the reflections, and the faith of a group of women who live and work in El Agustino, one of the poorest *barrios* (neighborhoods) of Lima, Peru. Such barrios were created by a massive influx of people into Lima from the 1960s to the present as Peruvians sought relief from the rampant poverty, the devastating violence of terrorism over the past three decades, and natural disasters.

The vast migration from rural areas to the cities, with the intermingling of different cultures, religious traditions, languages, and customs, has necessitated the rethinking of social structures. The new urban environment created the need to construct something new. This mass migration, and all it entails, creates a *mezcla* (mixture) of cultures and conditions unseen until this time. What does all this mean for the people, the church, and specifically the women of Peru? How, in turn, have the women of El Agustino responded?

We see in El Agustino the creation and evolution of a local theology born in the struggle to change the status quo while recognizing the presence of God. This theology arises from the bottom up, from the people and not from trained theologians. The actions of the women focused first and necessarily on the question of survival—survival for themselves, their families, and their community. Their theology focuses not on a worldwide transformation but rather on building and supporting societal structures to improve the local environment in response to the call of God.

The theological themes that emanate from the women of El Agustino emerge through their involvement with the institutional church, their work in various projects in the barrio, their family lives, and their prayerful reflections. These women for the most part do not possess much formal schooling. Nonetheless, they possess and espouse complex theological propositions with a high degree of independence and proficiency. A careful listening reveals a rich education of a different variety—one rooted in life-changing experiences.

Although the expression "to give voice" is used frequently in theological discourse today, I am admonished by the words of one El Agustino resident and coordinator of *La Federacíon Popular de Mujeres* (Federation of Women), Rosa Pacheco, who said to me: "You say you want to give voice to us women. Well, let me tell you this: women have always had a voice. The problem has been that the men who hold the power do not bother to listen to us. This, however, never stopped us from our mission."[1] Faith, perseverance, and the efficacy of love are lessons to be learned from the women of El Agustino.

Why These Women?

> *The expression, "women doing theology," is new, as is the explication of what the expression means. Previously, there was never any mention of sexual difference with regard to those who wrote theology, since it was obvious that the task was something proper to men. Today it would seem that the matter is no longer obvious, and the gender of the authors must be specified. Gender is understood not only as a biological difference prior even to birth, but especially as a cultural dimension, that is, as a stance or an aspect that affects*

the production of other cultural values, of other kinds of human interrelationship and other ways of thinking.

Ivone Gebara, S.N.D.
"Women Doing Theology in Latin America"

El Agustino is not the only barrio in which impressive action by women has occurred. In the *pueblo joven* (young or new town) of Villa El Salvador in Lima, a barrio very similar to El Agustino in its development, the NGO (nongovernmental or nonprofit organization) *La Federación Popular de Mujeres* (Women's Federation) plays an essential role in providing health care, food, and social services for the poor as well as acting as a very influential liaison with the city and federal governments and the local church.[2] Similar organizations were established in El Agustino and throughout the *pueblos jóvenes* of Lima. The impact of the work of women organizers is widespread and they share specific goals and sentiments throughout Peru in answer to the problems that they face.

One of the extraordinary early leaders of this movement was María Elena Moyano.[3] This dynamic, charismatic leader was born in 1958 in the Lima suburb of Barranco; her family moved to the *pueblo joven* of Villa El Salvador when she was thirteen. She studied psychology in college and emerged as a founder and leader of the Women's Federation in Villa El Salvador.

Sra. Moyano's social activism was dynamic and resulted in many positive changes for the poor. She actively fought lethargic and ineffective federal and local governments for improvements in housing, medical, food, and work programs. Her work, and the programs run by many people like her, threatened the nationwide anarchy plans desired by terrorist groups, especially *Sendero Luminoso* (Shining Path). If the poor experienced any improvement in their life conditions, the appeal of anarchy (and the allure of benefits promised by terrorists) were diminished. As a result, she received numerous death threats from Sendero. While Sendero was trying to tear apart the fabric of Peruvian society, women like Sra. Moyano struggled to hold life together and to move ahead. She lived very publicly and was the organizing force behind a massive protest against Sendero in Lima in September 1991. In February 1992, as she was leaving an organizing meeting, she was assassinated in front of her children.

The impact of her death was felt throughout Peru and more than three hundred thousand people attended her funeral. As Paulina Flores de Osorio, the founder of the *pueblo joven* of San Pedro, said, "The death of Elena had an impact on all of us—especially the women who are working for social change. In her life and death, we have a living example of what it means to be a Christian; to believe so deeply that you are ready to give up your life for the people of God. Is this not what Jesus did?"[4]

Maryknoll Sister Rosa Dominga Trapasso said,

> María Elena's death took on tremendous proportions because of how she was killed and what it meant. It exposed the vulnerability of everyone. It was a turning point for many people because Sendero could murder someone so close to the people. We were devastated by her death and the day of her funeral the Mass was concelebrated and, of course, it was all men. The irony was not missed. All the leftist politicians, some with their guns showing, were up in front, and the women with whom and for whom Elena worked—the vulnerable ones—were pushed to the back of the church and into the streets.[5]

Some of the women of El Agustino received death threats as well. This did not stop them from working for the betterment of the people in their district. Nor did these threats, a well as the innumerable obstacles they face daily, diminish their resolve to discover and understand more deeply the presence of God in their midst.

Why El Agustino?

> *You have to understand that just years ago there was nothing here in El Agustino: no streets, no trees, no electricity, no stores, no people. This was just a desolate area so close to downtown Lima but untouched by all that goes on in the city. And when people started to move here, it was more from necessity than desire. Who would want to live in such a dismal place? But most of us had no choice. So, we had no choice than to work very hard to create a place where life could go on, where children could be born and grow, where a glimmer of hope for the future could exist.*
>
> Edelmira Aclari Castellares
> Secretary at the neighborhood school

On the barren hills east of downtown Lima, once part of a large hacienda abandoned in the 1930s, a *Mercado Mayorista* (wholesale market) was built in 1945. As rural conditions in Peru deteriorated, people began to settle in this hilly, sparse, and inhospitable setting. New sections of the neighborhood arose almost overnight from these dusty, treeless, mostly uninhabited hills. Hundreds of Peruvians arrived in Lima weekly during the 1970s–1980s seeking economic security and freedom from violence. These exiles from their home districts entered Lima en masse. They built their homes from scrap wood and pieces of corrugated aluminum, carried water for miles from muddy streams, sewage flowed down ruts in the ground, electricity was a dream for the future, schools were nonexistent, hunger was the norm, and health problems ran rampant. This is the origin of El Agustino.

The Roman Catholic parish of *La Virgen de Nazaret* (The Virgin of Nazareth, commonly referred to as El Agustino) was created by then Cardinal Juan Landázuri Ricketts, the archbishop of Lima (1955–1990), in 1968 and was assigned to the Society of Jesus (Jesuits) in Peru. The parish would become a focal point for those struggling to make sense of the new and often threatening urban environment.

The women on whom this book focuses are residents of El Agustino. Many of them left the Peruvian countryside for Lima in the last three decades. Because of adverse conditions that brought them to the city and those they encountered upon their arrival, most of these new immigrants lived beneath the poverty level for many years. At some point, usually very soon after these women settled in El Agustino, they became involved in the projects of *Servicios Educativos El Agustino* (Educational Services El Agustino or SEA), the social outreach agency of *La Virgen de Nazaret* parish.

El Agustino in many ways represents the changes occurring throughout Lima and in each major city of the country and throughout Latin America from 1960 on. The mass internal migration patterns created entirely new civil, cultural, linguistic, and religious milieus. This influx of people into El Agustino also created massive problems to which the residents of the barrio, primarily the women, responded. This is the context in which theology is done. These are the context and the challenges to which the women respond.

Theologian Robert Schreiter wrote, "The poor are important because they give voice to the aspirations of what may be the majority of Christians in the world."[6] The women of Peru comprise half of the population. I turned to some of these women to hear their aspirations, challenges, successes, and defeats.

Liberation and Feminist Theologies

Although the women of SEA speak eloquently of the tenets, goals, and aspirations of Latin American liberation theology, for the most part they have little or no formal knowledge of this theological school. Yet, as Fr. Gustavo

Gutiérrez, the father of liberation theology, said, "They are the best of liberation theologians because they do not need the training. They live it; they live the Gospel."[7]

These women do not consider themselves liberation theologians, yet they share much in common with those who write and do research in this area. It is important to consider liberation theology because of its profound influence in Peru and worldwide as well as the question of what role women may play in its future developments. Gutiérrez, as early as 1960, was bringing together groups of poor women and men in Lima to discuss their relationship with God. His seminal work, *A Theology of Liberation*,[8] arose from this experience. Through his careful listening, he elaborated a theology of the people of God.[9]

Secular feminists in Peru—mostly upper class—are influenced by North American and European feminist theory. However, this influence has had a negligible impact upon the thinking of most of the women of El Agustino. The women in this study and the secular feminists of Peru share some of the same goals and aspirations despite the fact that the latter readily admit that there is little consideration of the plight of the poor in their writings, research, and reflections. As Dra. María Emma Mannarelli, a historian and administrator for *Centro de la Mujer Peruana Flora Tristan*[10] (Flora Tristan Peruvian Woman's Center), a leading secular feminist research institute, said, "I personally always have criticized this (lack of consideration of poor women) within Flora Tristan. . . . Not to address the question of poor women in a vertical society such as ours is a neglectful situation and one that must be corrected."[11]

The understandings central to Peruvian liberation theology and Peruvian secular feminism are something that the women of El Agustino instinctively embrace. Without any formal training in either liberation or feminist theologies, they speak of their desire for the fruits of both. Their social, cultural, and theological reflections bring to light the correlations between feminism and liberation theology.

However, this book is not meant to be either a comparison of feminist thought or the theological thinking of Peru's liberation theologians with the women of SEA. The theology of the women of El Agustino is not a subset of something that precedes it. This study is an examination of a theology emerging from women who are poor and who work for the poor.

These women experience lives permeated with hope for a new future—hope against hope, often in the direst of circumstances. As they compellingly speak of, and work toward, their dreams—for family, parish, neighborhood and neighbors, and country and world—their words, experiences, and ambitions stand in stark contrast to the individualism so common in the United States and Europe and among the wealthier citizens of their own country. As theologian James B. Nickoloff succinctly states, "The nascent solidarity among the poor—dramatically seen in

Peru, for example, when ethnic identity gradually gives way to a consciousness of social class—is the source of a genuine hope against the ubiquitous forces of death."[12]

These women have a profound sense that their faith, their hard work, and their love will most assuredly be able to achieve for them and for their neighbors the freedom they fervently desire, the liberation that the Gospel of Jesus Christ promises them. This liberation is all-encompassing. They work for freedom from the poverty that has crippled their lives and the lives of their families, neighbors, and friends; they look ahead to a time when the government of their country will truly have the welfare of its citizens—particularly its most vulnerable citizens—foremost among its goals; they foresee an era when the cultures of their ancestors stand in proud bearing with the implanted culture of the United States and the Iberian Peninsula; they anticipate a period when the barriers of a machismo society will no longer adversely influence their lives; they focus on building a liberating church that fully incorporates women and men as equals; and they work to lessen the economic, cultural, social, political, ecclesiastical, and personal obstacles that stand in the way of their living as fully human.

The women in this study represent the possibility of change for the better. Through their work and their faith, they help to redefine a theology of the poor, a theology for a liberating church. The themes of liberation of which they speak mirror the themes that are heard worldwide. However, as women whose voices have not been heard, as women who are quietly yet effectively changing the status quo, their goals are subtly different from other theologies and are very important. Indeed, in many ways the future of the church in Peru rests in the hands of the women of the church.

Contextual and Local Theologies

> *Contextualization . . . is the sine qua non of all genuine theological thought, and always has been.*
>
> Douglas John Hall
> *Thinking the Faith: Christian Theology in a North American Context*

Theologian Stephen B. Bevans provides the following definition of contextual theologies:

> Contextual theology can be defined as a way of doing theology in which one takes into account: the spirit and message of the Gospel; the tradition of the Christian people; the culture,

> whether brought about by Western technological process or the grass-roots struggle for equality, justice, and liberation. Doing theology contextually is not an option, nor is it something that should only interest people from the Third World or missionaries who work there. The contextualization of theology—the attempt to understand Christian faith in terms of a particular context—is really a theological imperative. As we understand theology today, contextualization is part of the very nature of theology itself.[13]

The time has come to hear the voices of the majority of Christians in the world and to explore the theological statements that reflect the reality in which this majority lives. It is also imperative that the contextual theologies be examined for patterns that will lead to a better understanding of how various issues are handled: fidelity to scripture and the magisterium (teaching authority of the Roman Catholic Church), the interplay of cultures, the role of women, and the manner in which context shapes the way in which we think and theologize. While classical theology thought of itself as an "objective science of faith,"[14] derived from the two sources of Scripture and tradition and therefore unchangeable, contextual theology adds a third *locus theologicus*, that of personal human experience. The subjectivity of this new way of faith seeking understanding rejects any consideration of a theology existing context-less. Our personal and communal realities are the only media through which we may come to an understanding of our God and our context inevitably influences that understanding.

The pluralistic and controversial nature of Christianity itself has been underappreciated in theological study for a long time. However, a cursory examination of Christian history attests to the fact that theology has always involved the process of trying to understand faith in a particular social, historical context. One need only compare the hierarchy of today's church with the early apostles to appreciate the manner in which culture has wielded its influence. As wars, reformation, politics, and reexamination of philosophy molded theology in the past, today the same occurs through the appreciation of the personal encounter with God. Clearly, the course of comprehending the Word of God made flesh continues and the holiness of the ordinary is recognized. The inherent pluralism of the world demands the attention of anyone doing theology if we believe in the Incarnation.

As we explore the spirit of the Gospel that is alive and flourishing in the lives of these women, when we come to a greater understanding of their Christian tradition and at the same time begin to grasp the *mezcla* (mixture) of cultures in which they live, there will emerge a local theology that may stand as a model for others.

Conclusion

In El Agustino, where everyone shares common poverty and displacement, the women's struggle is important because their inclusive efforts have allowed many to survive; it's significant by the movements of God in their midst made visible by their theological reflection; and it's meaningful for the example for others to follow and for the lessons Christians may share.

As the final document from the 1985 Oaxtepec, Mexico, Conference on "Doing Theology from Third World Women's Perspective" points out:

> The passionate and compassionate way in which women do theology is a rich contribution to theological science. The key to this theological process is the word "life." We perceive that women are deeply covenanted with life, giving life, and protecting life. The woman in our streets always appears surrounded and weighed down with children: children in her body, in her arms, on her back. Thus, even physically, she extends and reaches out to other lives, other human beings born of her body, sustaining their lives. In doing theology, we in the Third World thus find ourselves committed and faithful to all the vital elements that compose human life. Thus without losing its scientific seriousness, which includes analyzing the basic causes of women's multiple oppression, our theologizing is deeply rooted in experience, in affection, in life. We as women feel called to do scientific theology passionately, a theology based on feeling as well as on knowledge, on wisdom as well as on science, a theology made not only with the mind but also with the heart, the body, the womb. We consider this a challenge and an imperative not only for doing theology from women's perspective, but also for all theology.[15]

To understand the women of El Agustino, and their actions and their thoughts, we must examine the major factors that shape the context in which they live. Some of the most momentous social occurrences of this past century have brought them to this point. Their integral faith and how it moves them to a deeper, more complete understanding of their God will change the world in which they live. How they answer the call of God will lead them forward.

A typical street in El Agustino, with buildings
climbing the hills in the background.

CHAPTER 2

The Context

Peru today faces innumerable problems. Many of these are tied to the economy because the problem of poverty affects everything about life here. But we also have a beautiful country and loving, caring people who are not prepared to accept Peru as it is today. It is truly un pais de las maravillas *(a country of marvels) and wonderful things can and will happen. God has given us many resources and perhaps we are just learning how to use all of them.*

Ofelia Montes López
Director, Servicios Educativos El Agustino

Historical Reflection as a Foundation

El Agustino is built upon the traditions of the barrio, the city, the country, and the foreign cultures brought to, and assimilated into, Peruvian culture. We must understand this past and look for the theological and systemic links that have been carried forward. A historical perspective affords the opportunity to understand how a particular social, political, and theological environment has evolved and to grasp the many consequences.

A test of validity of a particular theology is whether it becomes the *sensus fidelium* (sense of the faithful). A community of faith must discern the truth in the concrete living out of the faith. This necessarily involves both an attention and faithfulness to tradition and a challenge to the same, just as it has been throughout the history of the church. In the case of El Agustino, the shining moments exist when the people respond passionately to their context and are able to state what the church, as an institution, and the people, as *communio fidei* (community of faith), need to hear.

In El Agustino a blend of the past and the present exists resulting in an ongoing conversation between the two. While living in one of the largest cities in the world, the people of El Agustino also preserve abundant traditional lifestyles brought there from throughout the country. The examination and the tackling of real-life issues often mean the difference between life and death. These issues negate the possibility of a theology that merely rethinks the dogmatic concerns of the past or that blindly accepts contemporary orthodoxy. The creative process of a local or contextual theology requires immersion into contemporary questions while simultaneously searching the past for answers.

Any theology must take seriously its obligation to struggle with the past and to come to an understanding of a complex present. The way in which a theology responds to the present is linked to what has been inherited. The traditions brought forth set a tone for all that will come. The women of El Agustino illustrate this in the movement toward the eradication of those traditions that are nonliberative, and in the undeviating emphasis on a faith that leads to human freedom. In their quest to build a liberating church, they also reaffirm liberating traditions that have been lost or underplayed through the centuries.

The theological process for these women involves the recognition of their responsibility to examine both the past and the present. Here we find a source of their hope. With that in mind, we will now more closely examine the past and present context out of which their theology arises. No theology emerges devoid of a context. Political, church, and social history must be examined to understand the source of a theology and where that theology leads the faithful.

Peru

The Republic of Peru, with an estimated population of 27.5 million in 2002, borders Ecuador and Colombia to the north, Brazil to the west, Bolivia to the southwest, and Chile to the south. The current borders contain a country slightly smaller than Alaska. When the Spanish arrived in 1531, the highly developed Inca civilization was centered here. With a nucleus at the city of Cuzco, the Incan empire covered a vast area from northern Ecuador to central Chile. Peru had been a center of artistic expression since pre-Columbian times, and the Inca people preserved these crafts and made remarkable accomplishments in architectural design.

The Spanish explorer Francisco Pizarro waged a ruinous war against the Inca people in his quest for gold. The conquerors captured Cuzco in 1533 and consolidated their control by 1542. Silver and gold from the Incas was the main source of wealth that paid for the Spanish invasion of the continent. Peru quickly became the focal point of power when Lima was founded by Pizarro in 1535. The viceroyalty established there had jurisdiction over all of South America except Brazil. Lima was an illustrious colonial capital and a Spanish stronghold by the time of the wars of independence (1820–1824).

However, the intervening two centuries led to the death of numerous native Peruvians by war and disease. Smallpox, measles, and even the common cold proved to be invincible enemies. The treasures so desired by the Spaniards began to run out and the invaders created a new base for the colonial economy, the *encomienda* system. Tracts of land were given to nobles and others by the Spanish monarchy. The *encomenderos* (the grantees), in turn, paid a heavy tribute to the monarch. The gift of land included the right to the labor of the people who lived on it. Thus, the freedom many Peruvians had known before the arrival of the Spaniards was abolished.

By the end of the eighteenth century, a yearning for independence was fueled by revolutions in the United States and in France. Juan Santos Atahualpa, a *meztizo* (person of mixed race), accompanied a Jesuit priest to Europe and was exposed to the ideas of revolution. He returned to Peru and founded a jungle community that expelled all Europeans from the area. The most famous of the revolutionaries was Tupac Amarú II, whose uprisings in the Cuzco area were a great embarrassment to the colonialists before he was brutally executed.

The 1814 defeat of Napoleon (and restoration of Spain's monarchy) weakened the Spanish government and it could no longer defend its colonies. In order to prevent Peru from resurging as a Spanish power base, revolutionary leaders Simon Bolívar and José de San Martín independently invaded Peru. San Martín had successfully led the Chilean fight for independence and moved up the coast toward Lima. He declared independence for Peru from Spain on 28 July 1821.

The first Peruvian parliament turned to Bolívar for leadership. After a mere two years as ruler, he departed Peru and chaos ensued. Almost two centuries of colonial rule, long and scattered battles for independence, weak leadership, shortage of food, and coups left the country in a poor state. Peru had thirty-five changes of government between 1827 and 1865.

Amid all of the transformations, little changed in the structure of Peruvian society. Those who had possessed power in colonial times continued to do so. And those who were poor before found themselves unable to battle successfully the social and economic systems that held them down.

A war with Chile (1879–1883) and the downfall of the Peruvian rubber market devastated the economy. Foreign creditors enforced stringent payback schedules and directly controlled many of the industries in the country. Working conditions imposed by foreign interests were deplorable. It wasn't until the 1920s that the workers began to organize. In 1924, Víctor Raúl Haya de la Torre, a Peruvian political activist, founded the *Alianza Popular Revolucionaria Americana* (*Aprista* Party[1] or Revolutionary Popular American Alliance, also referred to as APRA). In 1931, APRA first emerged as a political force in Peru among the majority of the popular classes and parts of the middle class. The more radical *Apristas* called for separation of church and state, the deportation of all foreign clergy, and the nationalization of church property. Haya de la Torre, the charismatic leader of APRA, quickly became a messianic-type leader who demanded absolute loyalty and created party functions that were closed off from the public. The popularity of the party began to spread, as did its anti-Catholic tendencies, and it came to be seen by some as a substitute for the Catholic religion—the religion that certain of the party's members felt oppressed the people. As Dra. Imelda Vega-Centeno wrote:

> What was created was the social construction of something real and credible, that is, produced from the initial political events (conversion and experience) but that finally would be consolidated into one, real religious-mythical figure through proclamation, teaching, and a utopian vision—that is, Haya de la Torre. Analysis of his speeches allows us to see the influence of a political gamble, the efficacy that this has in the party's historical and militant public image (through its code of practice), and its vision of the world: collective representation or myth being transmitted for the unconscious and collective memory.[2]

By the 1950s, APRA was regarded by many as too weak to handle the monumental problems of corruption, inflation, foreign interference, and domestic unrest. In 1956 Francisco Belaunde created the National Youth Front, later to be renamed *Acción Popular* (Popular Action). Although he was defeated by an alliance between the military and APRA, he reformed his ideas and was elected president in 1963. His influence was short-lived, due in no small part to his relationships with foreign oil corporations, and he was unseated by a bloodless military coup in 1968.

The new military leader, Gen. Juan Velasco, made far-reaching reforms by nationalizing the mining, gas, and fishing industries, handing over the estates of the oligarchy to the poor, and recognizing Quechua, the tongue of the Incas, as a second official language.

While Velasco's reforms were well received on many levels, the financial foundation of the country was too weak to handle the changes effectively. By 1975 he had lost the support of many factions of the country and was overthrown in another military coup. The people of Peru, however, had had enough and a short period of strikes, civil unrest, and spiraling inflation resulted in open elections being called. Haya de la Torre was elected president and he granted the vote to a majority of Peruvians who had previously been denied suffrage because of illiteracy. Belaunde, however, defeated him in 1980 and began a series of huge construction projects, such as roads that stretched across the Andes to the Amazon basin. These projects were crippled by the worsening economy, disastrous weather caused by *El Niño*, and the increasing activity of terrorist groups like *Sendero Luminoso* (Shining Path).

Belaunde lost the presidential election in 1985 to Alan Garcia, a young member of APRA. Garcia's tenure as president was undermined by charges of corruption, rising international debt, escalating inflation, and bloodshed throughout Peru caused by terrorist groups. The traditional political parties dismayed the country. This led to an eventual wave of support for Alberto Fujimori and his *Cambio* (Change) 90 Party against the noted writer Mario Vargas Llosa.

Fujimori, a former agricultural university rector, was elected president in 1990. His early years, although controversial, were successful in many ways. One of his early policies involved price controls and currency devaluation. Although this caused added hardship for the poor, they generally remained supporters because they felt he was taking the necessary steps. Some people actually called Fujimori the "George Washington" of Peru. The people did not approve of everything he did but the capture of the Sendero leadership led many to believe that the country had been born anew.

In 1992, in response to government corruption and to the intensifying terrorist activity, Fujimori declared an *autogolpe* (self-coup) and dissolved the congress and supreme court, giving himself more power. Later in 1992, his government captured the leader of Sendero, Abimael Guzmán Reynoso, and the country rallied around Fujimori. His reelection in 1995 came easily but his hold began to weaken.

Although he was able to circumvent the constitution and be reelected in 2000 to a third term, evidence of election tampering was revealed and the opposition boycotted the runoff. Human rights violations (illegal imprisonment, confiscation of property, government interference in the courts) were revealed daily in the Peruvian newspapers and the head of Fujimori's National Intelligence Service, Vladimiro Montesinos, was caught bribing an opposition lawmaker to influence a vote. In late 2000, the president fired Montesinos, who subsequently fled the country, was captured, and tried in Peru. Fujimori announced his resignation as soon as new elections took place. At this point, more than 80 percent of the country favored his departure and he left for a trip to Japan, from where he sent a resignation letter to the congress.

A caretaker government oversaw new elections in the spring of 2001, which ushered in Alejandro Toledo as the new head of government. The *mestizo* former shoe shiner with a doctorate from Stanford University became president in July 2001. Already, his presidency is tarnished by accusations that he is not able to lead the country forward. He stylized himself as a successor of Pachacuti ("cataclysm" or "destroyer"), a fifteenth-century Incan emperor who expanded and unified the Inca Empire, and this appealed to the poor, his most fervent supporters but alienated many others.

Sendero Luminoso

> *No one can imagine the horror of never knowing when Sendero would strike again. I guess that was their biggest means of success. Just when you thought life might be returning to normal, a bomb would explode or someone would be assassinated. We all spent a great deal of time and energy trying to make sense of the senseless. We all spent a great deal of time worrying about ourselves, our families, our neighbors.*
>
> Margarita Córdova Herrera
> Director
> SEA's *Bancos Comunales*
> (Communal Banks)

The people of Peru lived in a peripatetic culture of violence and fear during the height of Sendero activity. Terrorism completely fractured and paralyzed the country of Peru and provoked changes in the way in which most Peruvians lived.

Sendero had its origins in the Peruvian *altiplano* (high-altitude plateau) in the 1960s. Guzmán,[3] known to his followers as Presidente Gonzalo, originally founded the clandestine Red Faction within the Peruvian Communist Party. However, after Guzmán's arrest in 1969, he was expelled from the party and subsequently spent eleven months in jail. Upon his release in 1970, the Red Faction became known as the Shining Path.

Sendero was one of the most effective, terrifying, and mystifying Latin American armed organizations.[4] Thus, any contemporary review of the state of Peru must begin with a discussion of this violent, Maoist, armed, left-wing organization. This background also is key to understanding the profound changes in the city of Lima, the concurrent growth of the barrio of El Agustino, and the impact these have on women.

The remote and impoverished Peruvian *departamento* (province or state) of Ayacucho was the birthplace of Sendero. It is also the home of an isolated, politicized, and ideologically radical university, *La Universidad de San Cristóbal de Huamanga*. The peasant struggle for the control of land owned by wealthy ranchers and corporations between 1960 and 1980 was at the forefront of Sendero's initial fight, but equally tumultuous was the cry for free education—educational opportunities that were constantly being reduced by the then-military government.[5]

La Universidad de San Cristóbal de Huamanga was founded in 1677 but it was closed between 1885 and 1959. Despite the government's attempt to eliminate most of the university courses after its reopening, Ayacucho became a center for the study and spread of radical thought. As the revolutionary fervor rose, so did the incidents of terrorism and coercion.[6] The students came to believe more fervently in what they were learning, and their desire to spread the revolution grew. The acts of violence grew in abundance, and the number of people fleeing the province, in order to preserve life and livelihood, did as well.[7] "Ayacucho and the neighboring provinces of Huancavelica and Apurímac were the greatest net generators of rural flight to Peruvian cities (essentially Lima). . . . Therein lies the explanation of how Sendero broke out of the Andean highlands."[8] The *campesinos* fled the department of Ayacucho, as did many *senderistas* (members of Sendero) who departed, seeking to spread the movement.

To comprehend fully the origins and expansion of Sendero, one must first look at the condition of the *campesinos* and *campesinas* (peasants or farmers) of the rural areas of the country, most of whom are of Indian descent. From the sixteenth century, when the Spanish invaders debated whether or not the indigenous population was fully human,[9] until the present, this large segment of the Peruvian population has never been incorporated into the economic, political, social, and ecclesiastical functions of the country. Therefore, when Guzmán and his followers appealed for support from those who were the most oppressed in Peru, the response at first was enthusiastic. Sendero had spent more than fifteen years organizing the movement before its armed struggle was launched. The iron discipline of Gúzman was attractive to many, particularly the disaffected students of the area.

> Little did the campesinos or the left-wing liberal supporters of Sendero know when they joined forces with Guzmán, that to support Sendero would mean committing atrocities against innocent civilians caught in the middle of this madness. Even fewer suspected that the slightest criticism of Guzmán's political ideologies and guerilla strategies would lead to their own deaths.[10]

In its earliest years (1970–1980), Sendero was a regional organization that espoused radical rhetoric but that remained essentially nonviolent. It claimed to be Maoist in its foundation,[11] but this proved to be more lip service than the basis of its ideology. Sendero's creation in the *departamento* of Ayacucho was a decisive factor in its success. The people initially turned to Sendero as a beacon of hope in the midst of the dire poverty in which they existed. Ayacucho remains the second poorest of Peru's *departamentos* and its citizens are indeed among the poorest of the poor.

Shining Path turned to the cities, in particular Lima, with a well-planned dream of anarchy.[12] In March and April of 1982, Sendero blacked out Lima through simultaneous destruction of electrical power lines and then detonated numerous explosions under the cover of darkness. At the time of the first assault on the capital, the Ayacucho prison also was attacked and 247 people, many of them Sendero's principal leaders, were freed. It had now become obvious to many people, but not so to the military or government, that Sendero was an ominous foe. As James D. Rudolph, a resident of Peru during those years, writes:

> The attendance of between 10,000 and 30,000 people at the Ayacucho funeral of 19-year-old slain senderista Edith Lagos in September (of 1982) demonstrated that the insurgents had gained the backing of considerable numbers of the local population. This conclusion was supported by numerous estimates at the time by journalists, scholars, and even the police chief of Ayacucho that Sendero had gained the allegiance, whether through admiration or fear, of a large majority of the citizens of Ayacucho, particularly among its youth.[13]

As Sendero's presence began to be felt in Lima and throughout the country in the early 1980s, the economy of Peru continued to worsen. This was indicative of the economic climate of all of Latin America at the time, yet the flight of investors and capital and the uncertainty of the future stability of the government and the free market exacerbated the situation in Peru. By 1982, the year Sendero's presence began to touch life in the capital city, the inflation rate had reached an annual rate of 320%. By 1990 it had reached a staggering 7,650%,[14] unemployment was estimated at 36%,[15] the crime rate was escalating exponentially, homelessness abounded, and hundreds of people were fleeing weekly from rural areas into the city.

"Official figures show that the economic damage attributed to political violence—principally Sendero—between 1980 and 1990 was more than $18 billion; that is six times the value of total annual exports, or the equivalent of 80 percent of Peru's foreign debt."[16] Vega-Centeno states that "this was a period in which the NGOs (non-governmental organizations or non-profits) and government social services were completely unprepared to handle the massive influx of new people, and the military government seemed just perplexed by the advent of the violent actions of the terrorists in a place, Lima, that had previously seemed protected."[17]

Popular confidence was growing after Fujimori was elected president in 1990 and his government imprisoned Guzmán and much of the leadership of Sendero in 1992.[18] However, the invasion of the Japanese ambassador's residence and the subsequent holding of forty-two Peruvian and foreign national hostages by the *Movimiento Revolucionario Tupac Amarú* (Revolutionary Movement Tupac Amarú or MRTA) in December of 1996 raised doubts that Fujimori had the terrorist situation under control.

Even after the Sendero movement appeared fatally weakened by the incarceration of its guiding forces and the successful rescue of the MRTA hostages in April of 1997, Francisco Chamberlain, S.J., current pastor of El Agustino says, "The people of Peru still wait for the next paralyzing explosion of terrorist activity that will plunge the country back into the chaos of the 1980s."[19] Under the current leadership of President Toledo, it is not uncommon to hear people on the streets wonder if signs of Sendero are appearing again. There is always the suspicion that all that happened before could plague the country again. The collective psyche of the nation, particularly that of its urban dwellers, is profoundly affected by this expectation. This potential threat is constantly lying just beneath the surface, as Fr. Gustavo Gutiérrez said "because we (Peruvians) have grown accustomed to acts of violence striking just when you think it is all over. It is like living in a war zone where no one tells you when and where the war will start up again."[20]

The Church in Peru

> *The church here in El Agustino has established a space in which women can say what they feel and be listened to. But I speak of the church here and not the church throughout the country or the world. For example, here in El Agustino, there is more freedom to speak about the control of one's reproductive bodies than there exists in wealthier parishes. I understand this from my meetings throughout the city (of Lima). However, I ask, "why is there not a space where women can say what they feel about reproductive rights everywhere?" There is manipulation here that is old in the church. So I hope, I pray, I continue to work. And I believe that God hears me; hears us. I guess patience is necessary. But when is the church going to do what it says* we *should do? That is, when*

is the church going to admit that it has made a mistake and many people have been hurt because of it? I sometimes wonder if the men in Rome have any idea of how life is lived in the "El Agustinos" of the world.

Benedicta "Beni" Serrano Agüero
Executive Director
Comedores Populares
(Communal Dining Rooms)

The most enduring legacy of Spanish colonization in Peru is the prevalence of Roman Catholicism. The impact of Peru's official religion is felt at all levels of society: political, social, economic, and of course, religious. While many of the cultures and languages of the conquered people survive today,[21] the Spanish Catholic culture predominates. Thus, it is essential to look at this cultural Catholicism so as to understand the Peru of today and the people of El Agustino.

The Colonial Period—1532–1821

Whereas the evangelization of Peru was considered complete by the middle of the seventeenth century, the assimilation of Catholicism often was accomplished in a localized fashion. The indigenous population responded to those aspects of the imported religion that most appealed to their particular desires and needs. For example, as noted Latin American church historian Jeffrey Klaiber, S.J. writes, "Andean Catholicism blended communitarian festivity with stoic resignation, reverence for the *Pachamama* (Mother Earth) with deep devotion to the Virgin Mary, Christ and the saints, ritual (and collective) drinking at funerals with deep and prayerful participation in the liturgy."[22]

A concrete example of this inculturation comes from a mural of the crucified Christ painted by an anonymous African slave in 1641. After the mural survived a devastating earthquake, it was christened *El Señor de los Milagros* (the Lord of Miracles). The section of the wall that survived is paraded through the streets to this day and revered in all levels of society in Peru.[23]

Peru also had four saints canonized from the colonial period: Rosa de Lima,[24] Martín de Porres,[25] Toribio de Mogrovejo,[26] and Francisco Solano[27]—whose canonizations added to an already fervent devotion to the saints. All of these proclivities remain a part of worship style today as evidenced by ceremonies conducted in El Agustino.

Spanish jurisdictional authority was decreased by the *criollo* (African Peruvian) and Indian rebellions of the eighteenth century and was eventually overthrown by Simon Bolívar (*el liberador* or "the Liberator") in 1824. Emancipation was completed in December 1824 when Gen. Antonio José de Sucre defeated the Spanish troops at Ayacucho, ending Spanish rule in South America. Spain made futile attempts to regain its former colonies, but in 1879 it finally recognized Peru's independence. The Spanish legacy lived on, however, especially in the church.

The Church after Independence—1821–1929

When Peru declared itself a republic in 1821, Roman Catholicism was proclaimed the official religion to the exclusion of all others. Additionally, the Spanish influence survived in the church due to a shortage of native-born priests, due to the lack of training opportunities and little outreach to Peruvian men. "By the late 1880s about 60 percent of the clergy in Peru . . . were foreign-born missionaries."[28]

As more members of religious orders arrived in Peru,[29] they founded schools, a university, orphanages, parishes, and social service agencies. A valid criticism of the religious schools then was that their upper-class and elitist student bodies and atmospheres were exclusionary. Even today, the most prestigious schools, those whose enrollments are comprised of the middle and upper classes, are operated by religious orders in Peru. By contrast, the "rural" church located in the jungle, coastal, and Andean regions—that is, those areas that would be the source of the massive urban migration in the late twentieth century—continued to be the primary source of cultural and historical reference. In these places, there existed ecclesiastical accommodation to the social intractability and to the resistance to change inherent in these areas. In other words, ". . . the church was widely accepted in that (rural) world precisely because it adjusted itself to the style of life there. . . . Historically, one discovers in Catholicism a firmness with regard to dogma and doctrine, but at the same time an elastic flexibility when it comes to pastoral practice."[30]

A worldview, existing then and now among the indigenous population, was documented by anthropologist George Foster in 1965. He described this worldview of rural residents as one of a prevalent fatalism in which all that was necessary for life would always be limited. Due to the peasant mentality that this would always be the case, the rural resident did not possess any strong will to work harder to change the status quo.[31] It was not until the 1930s that the church helped create an environment in which a change of attitude flourished.

The church began to establish a reputation for being the defender of the peasants in the first century of independence. Rural (and mostly foreign) priests were the primary motivators for bringing educational opportunities to the countryside. Later, the church formed the *Congreso de acción social* (Congress of Social Action or CAS) that was convened in Cuzco in 1921. The bishops also began to play an important role in Indian relations with the creation of the "Patronage of the Indian Race," a governmental body whose function was to hear Indian complaints. Officials of the church continued to create structures to protect the Indians against abuse on numerous levels.

The Tumultuous 1930s—and Beyond

The development of APRA had profound implications for the church. The demand by *Apristas* for the separation of church and state, deportation of foreign clergy, and the nationalization of church property caused turmoil in ecclesiastical circles. The church felt besieged in an environment in which it had long enjoyed political, religious, and social influence and power. On a positive note, the church hurried to create a more well-formed and educated laity, which would be capable of responding to disaffection stirred up by APRA.

As a result, the Peruvian church employed the idea of "Catholic Action" a number of years before Pope Pius XI (1922–1939) popularized the expression in 1931. The Peruvian church (and the Pope) dealt with the subject of how Christians should work to improve the life of the poor, disenfranchised, and disheartened here on earth. This went up against a popular sense that one must "offer up to God" any earthly suffering in order to achieve a heavenly reward. Although the Peruvian church's concept of "Catholic action" in the early 1930s focused almost exclusively on the defense of ecclesiastical authority, the outcome of its call for social action was the formation of numerous organizations that focused on the issues of human rights (some of these organizations still exist) and the creation of a "social activist mentality" within the church that is carried forth today.[32]

Amid these societal and political changes, an intellectual awakening was fermenting in the church. Spurred on by the ongoing development of the *Pontificia Universidad Católica del Perú* (Pontifical Catholic University of Peru or PUC, founded in 1917), Catholic intellectuals began to have a national impact.[33] This transitional period was laying the foundation for the metamorphosis of the church in Peru.

The Modernization of the Peruvian Church

The church in Peru underwent many transformations and advancements between 1955 and 1975. Jeffrey Klaiber S.J. subdivides these periods into "the modern church" [1955–1968] and "the social-political church" [1968–1975].

A Church Facing Modernity—1955–1968

The most dramatic changes in the church came with the appointment of Juan Landázuri Ricketts as archbishop of Lima in 1955 and as cardinal-prelate of Peru in 1962. Under his administration, the *Oficina nacional de la educación católica* (National Office of Catholic Education or ONDEC) was founded in 1955, the *Conferencia de los religiosos* (Conference of Religious) in 1956, and the *Conferencia de las monjas* (Conference of Women Religious) in 1963. In 1955, the first meeting of the Latin American bishops (*Consejo Episcopal Latinoamericano* or CELAM) was held in Rio de Janeiro, Brazil.

Under Landázuri's dynamic leadership, the church in Peru began to open itself to dialogue with the Western world, engage in conversations about pluralism, integrate the social sciences into its analyses and formation policies, and encourage Catholic intellectual development.

Between 1955 and 1969, a large number of foreign missionaries arrived with a vision of how the church was to be transformed, particularly in the light of Vatican II (1962–1965). A notable political factor present during this period was the *Partido democristiano* (Christian Democratic Party or PDC), whose members came to represent Christians of Peru whose political agenda promoted a strong social awareness.

In 1957, Landázuri created *La Misión de Lima* (The Mission of Lima) to serve the pastoral and social requirements of the *pueblos jóvenes* (then called *barriadas* or "slums").[34] At that time, there were 120,000 residents in the *pueblos jóvenes*, and *La Misión* created satellite chapels, medical facilities, meeting rooms for neighborhood organizers, and centers for mothers.[35]

The Peruvian bishops' pastoral letter of 1958, under the tutelage of Landázuri, reversed their previous trend of writing and speaking of creating a just social order but never attacking the systemic injustices that created the problems. The 1958 epistle called for the Christians of Peru to unite in order to change an unjust society. It even went so far as to signify the aggregation of wealth by the oligarchy as one source of social ills.[36]

With the pastoral letter came the *Primera Semana Social* (the First Social Week) during which priests, religious, and laity met for the first time to analyze the social ills plaguing the country and to determine a course of action for the church. This meeting served multiple functions: It brought to light in realistic terms the immensity of the problems; it served as a training vehicle in social analysis for religious and lay workers; it assisted in integrating organizations and eliminating the duplication of efforts; and it acted as a very effective arm of the church in bringing the plight of the poor to the attention of the general population of Peru.

The Social-Political Church—1968–1975

The *Consejo Episcopal Latinoamericano* (Council of Latin American Bishops or CELAM) meeting at Medellín, Colombia, in August and September of 1968, initiated a crucial period for the Latin American church. The efficacious emphasis of the Latin American church on social action and on the plight of the poor, so strongly advocated at this meeting, carries forth to this day. This occurs despite efforts to return to a pre-Vatican II church so desired by conservative Catholics in Peru and throughout Latin America.

The names of the principal documents issued by the bishops at the Medellín CELAM—documents on justice, peace, and poverty—clearly indicate the directions in which they desired their church to go.[37] Their document, "Commitments to the Latin American Church," concisely outlines their objectives: new order of justice; promotion of the efficacy of the family; increase of dynamic, preparatory education; workers' rights; new evangelization; new ecclesiastical structures to increase dialogue between the laity and religious; and ecumenical discussions.[38]

After CELAM in Medellín, many of the missionary groups in Peru underwent a self-evaluation both to meet the provisions of CELAM and to determine the legitimacy of their own presence. Part of the impetus for the latter concern was the article published by Fr. Ivan Illich[39] titled "The Seamy Side of Charity," in which he warned against the increasingly large numbers of priests, brothers, and religious being sent to Latin America.[40] While acknowledging the good intentions of the missionaries, he asserted that the swell of immigrant religious in the 1960s constituted a threat to the possibility of the church in Latin America undergoing its own evolution.

Dom Hélder Câmara, the Brazilian archbishop who was a moving force behind CELAM in Medellín, wrote just two years later: "Instead of planning to go to the Third World to try to arouse violence there, stay at home in order to help your rich countries to discover that they too are in need of a cultural revolution which will produce a new hierarchy of values, a new world vision, a global strategy of development, the revolution of mankind."[41] For the first time, foreign priests, nuns, and brothers were examining the many layers of motivation that brought them to Peru in the first place. While the church in Peru did have problems, the presence of so many foreigners did not facilitate the examination of church direction needed at this time. A Northern Hemisphere concept of what the Peruvian church should be had crept into the psyche of the church of Peru. In addition, the aftermath of Vatican II was turbulent. There was a decrease in vocations and the discussion over how the social agenda of Medellín should be implemented caused much division.

The Church, the Military, and Social Change

At the same time that the problems of domestic migration were erupting on the scene in Peru, the country was also dealing with the reformist military regime of Gen. Juan Velasco Alvarado (1968–1975). The aftermath of Vatican II, the social encyclicals of John XXIII and Paul VI,[42] the Medellín CELAM, the increase of political activity on the part of peasants in the Andes, as well as the presence of a military government were all compelling the church in Peru to reexamine most of its policies. Priests and laypeople formed the *Oficina nacional de información social* (National Office of Social Information or ONIS) and actively decried the systemic social injustices that crippled the lives of people in Peru. ONIS became a moving force in publicly criticizing the military for its human rights violations.

The *Comisión episcopal de acción social* (Bishops Commission of Social Action or CEAS)[43] was founded in 1965. It became the principal means by which the bishops were informed of the social dilemmas upon which they should act. As Bishop Luis Bambarén Gastelumendi, S.J., the former bishop of the *barriadas* and the first head of CEAS, said:

> CEAS performed two very crucial functions. First of all, that of keeping the hierarchy of the church informed of the social problems that were stymieing the social action of the church in Peru—action instigated by (the CELAM meeting in) Medellín. This was a profound change because all levels of the church—from bishops to the laity in upper-class parishes—were hearing firsthand the problems facing the people of God, some for the first time. And this leads into the second function: that of hearing the voices of the people. This had a twofold affect: first, hearing and acknowledging the problems; second and equally important, giving the people a sense of their own authority, a sense that the church was really listening to them and acknowledging their agency. This in turn encouraged more and more social action groups to form and grow in the *pueblos jóvenes*. This has had lasting affects.[44]

While the church did not openly approve of the presence of the military government, it did support the measures initiated by the military to reform unjust structures.[45] Instances of cooperation, at times an odd relationship, also existed. For example, *La Ley de reforma educativa* (the Educational Reform Law) of 1972 was the result of the discourse between the church and the military. This new law enabled the church to begin staffing numerous schools in poorer areas.[46] The liberation theology "summer courses" offered at the PUC starting in 1971 and the founding of the *Instituto Bartolomé de Las Casas* by Gutiérrez in 1974 provided educational opportunities for all levels of society.[47]

The 1979 CELAM in Puebla de los Ángeles, Mexico, although fraught with divisions not found at Medellín, "created a road map for the social programs of the church. Archbishop (Alfonso López) Trujillo[48] rallied the conservative forces of the Latin America church but, in the end, this worked against him. The people of Latin America were not ready to have the social agenda of the church thrown out with the trash."[49] The Peruvian delegation, headed by Cardinal Landázuri,[50] presented a strong, united force at the conference. Pope John Paul II was present at the Puebla conference and he did not condemn liberation theology as many conservatives hoped he would do. Instead, the Pope issued a strong denunciation of social injustice in Latin America[51] and the substance of the Medellín social agenda was reaffirmed.

The New Evangelization

In the 1980s, as the quincentenary of the arrival of Spanish missionaries in Latin America approached, the previous and present eras were reexamined with a critical eye to the new challenges being delivered to the church of the future. The roots of this process of commemoration and examination are to be found in the documents of Vatican II, Medellín, Puebla, the Peruvian bishops' letter on evangelization in 1973, as well as the exhortation of the papal encyclical *Evangelii nuntiandi* (1975).

In the Peruvian bishops' letter of 1973, they declared that evangelization proclaims the good news of the life of Jesus Christ and that this must effectively result in historical and social action, which will transform the world in light of the Gospel. The raison d'être of the church is the proclamation of this good news and this involves three moments: declaration and denunciation, testimony, and transformative praxis. Hanii Rolfes, a German theologian, member of the Missionaries of the Sacred Heart, and professor of theology at the *Instituto Superior de Estudios Teológicos* (Higher Institute of Theological Studies) in Lima, describes these moments:

> This signifies that the church must announce the good news with acts and words: words that proclaim the love of God and the strength of God's reign among humankind, that reveal the presence of Jesus Christ the liberator in human life; words that denounce all that is opposed to this reign and negate the presence of God. And at the same time, in order to give concrete expression and truth to these words: acts of effective service in the promotion of human dignity and in the process of the his-

> torical liberation of the people. They are acts and words that confirm and explicate each other mutually.
>
> Similarly, a total liberating evangelization seeks to realize a living synthesis of announcement, of testimony and of action. It proclaims Jesus Christ as king of justice, love, truth, liberty, fellowship, and of commitment to transformative action in the world that actualizes the message of the word of God; the realization of the reign of God through a struggle of solidarity for a more fraternal society, and with a testimony of a quality of life and a model of living together in a more human fashion. . . .[52]

The new evangelization was one of the ongoing events that sanctioned a novel perception of the contemporary reality of Latin America for Christians. It facilitated the movement toward new methodologies in the process of making real and present the word of God. In this fashion, there may be discovered again a means of changing the mentality of the faithful. This permeated the thinking of the women of El Agustino. They were not merely aware of these various documents and exhortations. The women understood the importance of this movement, studied the documents, and worked to implement the word of Jesus Christ who advocated "justice, love, truth, liberty, fellowship, and commitment to transformative action in the world." "We are well aware of the negative effects of the evangelization brought by the Spanish," said Rosa Canto Castro, a community organizer, "and we hope now to bring the word of God to people in totally liberating ways."[53]

The Conservative Church

Despite the emphasis of the Peruvian church on social action and on its integration into theological thinking since the 1950s, it would be naive to think that this is a response supported by all of the church's members. The conservative church in Peru exhibits little concern for social realities and presents itself in the model of the authoritarian and dogmatic institution that thrived worldwide before the Second Vatican Council. It yearns for the reestablishment of the past with its locus on the insular concepts of morality and "proper" Catholic upbringing. In the documents and writings of conservatives in Peru, there is only an "obligatory" reference to human rights or social development. This appears necessary (albeit in a quite restricted fashion) as an oblique acknowledgment of the profound presence that the social movements have among the faithful.

Defending against the perceived threat to the central authority of the church is the major motivating factor behind the conservative movements in Peru today. First, the formation of theological trends outside of the usual ecclesiastical or intellectual circles is verboten. Second, any theology's implicit association with Marxism or socialism is reason enough for condemnation by some members of the hierarchy. The 1984 "Instruction on Certain Aspects of the Theology of Liberation" of the Congregation for the Doctrine of the Faith justified the censure of Marxist analysis because "atheism and the rejection of the human person, of his freedom and his rights, are at the center of the Marxist conception."[54]

Marxism, however, was utilized by the liberation theologians as a means of social critique, and the theologians stridently opposed the Marxist concepts of materialism.[55] The Marxism adopted by theologians in Peru and elsewhere is what theologian Enrique D. Dussel labeled *theoretical Marxism.*

> This is the Latin American sociological and economic Marxism of "dependency". . . . It is this sociology of dependency, with its criticism of functionalism and developmentalism that will occasion the epistemological breach on the part of the theology of liberation. . . . Marxism is also found indirectly among the pertinent social sciences as an instrument for the discovery and description of the poverty of the Latin America people and the concrete projects of liberation.[56]

Marxism and the Downfall of Socialism

The oligarchy firmly controlled the political, social, and economic scene throughout Peru by the beginning of the twentieth century. Nevertheless, this century also saw several political alternatives presented to the people. The *indigenista* (indigenous) uprisings gave birth to various Indian groups that worked for equality with the mostly European owners of land and factories. Socialism began to touch the working environment by the turn of the century as the increase of the working class coincided with the movement away from subsistence farming.

The use of Marxist analysis on the part of Latin American theologians (and others throughout the world) is problematic. Moreover, there was no consistent agreement over what the use of Marxist analysis actually meant. The essence of the question remains whether or not one may use elements of Marxist analysis without ascribing to all of the Marxist tenets, in particular its atheism. Many theologians and other people of faith appreciate the reasons why certain tenets of Marxism are both attractive and applicable to the current social environments in the world. The church and numerous religious figures have cried out for the care of the poor and disenfranchised. Their appeal for the promotion of justice often resembles that of avowed Marxists. On the other hand, the primacy of Marxism worldwide has abated. The question arises, what influence does the fall of socialism have on Peru?

The identification of Marxist analysis with liberation theology still haunts its proponents. The admonitions of the Vatican's Congregation for the Doctrine of the Faith concerning the links between Latin America liberation theology and Marxist ideology substantiate this difficulty.[57] The link between any identification with Marxism and its stand on atheism worries the Roman hierarchy.

Globalization

The move away from socialism ushered in the era of globalization. One may ask how the factors of globalization could affect the poor and disenfranchised in an impoverished and underdeveloped neighborhood in Lima, Peru. Lima certainly is not one of the global cities that economists and analysts of globalization are discussing.[58] It is not a center for international commerce and production. Yet the phenomenon of globalization is reaching all parts of the world and is influencing societies worldwide in a variety of ways. The effects of globalization are also touching the lives of the people of El Agustino.

First, however, we must define what we mean by *globalization*. Although it is a frequently used term in today's world, there does not appear to be a commonly accepted definition. Robert J. Schreiter contends that, although there is no one accepted interpretation, most would agree. "It is about the increasingly interconnected character of the political, economic, and social life of the peoples of the planet."[59] It is not necessary to be a Marxist to understand that economic factors exercise a dynamic role in the development of the cultural, political, social—and theological—contexts of a country.

G. B. Madison, professor emeritus of philosophy at the Institute on Globalization and the Human Condition at McMaster University, Ontario, Canada, explains:

> The very term *civilization* has a dual material/spiritual significance, and in the advance of civilization the material and the spiritual are always conjoined. The history of civilization is the history of its progressive liberation from material deprivation, i.e. of economic development, and it is the history as well of the growth of freedom in the realm of the spirit. We now have a name for the dynamics at work in the present stage in the development of civilization: globalization.

> The phenomenon of globalization is itself global, that is to say, all encompassing. It is of course in the first instance a material or economic phenomenon, but, like all significant civilizational developments, it also has profound cultural or spiritual significance. Nothing in human affairs is ever merely economic.[60]

In his discussion of the globalization process in the context of theology, Schreiter outlines the demise of state socialism, the worldwide expansion of capitalism, and the advent of neoliberalism.[61] While this process has generated unforeseen amounts of wealth, this has decidedly not "trickled down" but rather has driven much of the world's population deeper into poverty while the wealthy become more so.

There is a leveling of cultural differences as well, a result of consumerism in a worldwide market that homogenizes lifestyles throughout the world. In essence, the process of globalization has spread the effects of modernity throughout the world, even to those areas that are less than grateful recipients. On a positive note, this process has created the possibility of more wealth being available for education and social programs. On the other hand, the definition of personhood has become more defined by one's capability to produce and consume the products that cross international boundaries in huge quantities, largely from the First World to the Third. A stroll through El Agustino graphically confirms this occurrence in the wardrobes, hairstyles, foods, and music one encounters.

How, then, does the meaning of context change vis-à-vis globalization? For Peru, for Lima, and especially for El Agustino, the context has itself changed dramatically and this by necessity modifies the manner in which theology is done. The contextual theologies that arose during the 1970s stood in contrast to the "universal" theologies—theologies that were not universal for a majority of the population of the world. The development of more recent theologies is an attempt to take into consideration the life-shaping forces that were at work in these persons' lives; that is, to answer the question, Where and how is God present in a particular time and place? As the world rapidly changes and as these modifications begin to impact people in even the most isolated areas, it is imperative when considering contextual theology to take note of these radically altered environs.

For the people of El Agustino, there was the dramatic influx of many cultural groups in large numbers, the ensuing poverty heightened by the national debt, the worldwide economic crises with the ever-widening gap between the rich and the poor, the cultural implantation from the colonial era together with that from the United States enhanced by technological advancement, as well as the pervasive threat of terrorism. The context of

El Agustino has been transfigured fundamentally. This is the contemporary context in which theology must be done.

The City of Lima and the Barrio of El Agustino

The Impact of Internal Migration

Estimates indicate that Peru had an estimated population of 27.5 million in 2002. Of this number, 49.7% (13,667,500) are female and 52% (7,107,100) of the women live below the poverty level.[62] The city of Lima will have grown from a half-million inhabitants in 1940[63] to 9 million in 2003. Of this number, 49% live below the poverty level.[64] Nothing has prepared the municipal or federal governments for this type of growth or the immensity of the problems they face.

More than any other Peruvian city, the capital has been burdened with the need to respond to this massive growth. During the height of the Sendero years (1982–1992), attempts on the part of federal and municipal governments to provide a minimum of services to the new immigrants were hampered by the terrorists' repeated destruction of electrical, telecommunications, water, and sewage facilities in Lima.[65] The strategy of Sendero kept the poor dissatisfied and thereby increased the appeal of their anarchic dreams. The government's rejoinder was to respond only to those who held the most influence and money. The poor, who had left most of their possessions and their livelihood behind in their home provinces, found themselves in subhuman conditions with little hope for the future. It was only when the voting power of the poor was recognized and mobilized[66] that the presidential candidate Alberto Fujimori began to make promises about improvements in services to the poorest barrios. This was not a purely altruistic move. Fujimori and his advisors realized that he was considered a political outsider in Peru and he decided to capitalize on this by appealing to the poor who also considered themselves outsiders.

Lima has been the capital of Peru since the Spanish founded it in 1535, and it dominates the social, cultural, political, and religious life of the country. While this is home to Peru's wealthiest citizens, numerous studies attest to the fact that it now ranks higher in poverty than any other *departamento* of Peru.[67] Although poverty is rampant throughout the country, the destitution experienced by the poor in Lima is very often a question of life or death. Subsistence farming, often the only means of staying alive in the rural areas, is not a choice. The extended family system so prominent in the countryside is not available for child- or eldercare.

At the same time, certain sections of the country prospered. Henry Dietz, a professor of government at the University of Texas, published a twenty-year study of urban poverty in Peru. In it, he reveals,

> Throughout the period in question (1970–90), Lima's grip on virtually all indicators of economic, social, and physical well-being remained solid. In the mid-1980s, Lima produced 69 percent of the nation's industrial output and 80 percent of its consumer goods. Lima generated 87 percent of Peru's tax revenues; possessed 98 percent of its private investment; received 83 percent of its bank deposits; and contained more than half its public employees, half its hospital beds, three-quarters of its telephone subscribers, while being home for 28 percent of its population.

Those who have financial resources and influence were able to live quite comfortably and even thrive at times. However, Dietz continues:

> Open unemployment rose from 5 percent in 1987 to 8 percent in 1990; underemployment (defined as either working less than thirty-five hours a week or receiving less than the minimum wage) increased over the same two years from 35 to 81 percent. By the end of the 1980s, income inequalities had become more profound than ever: the poorest (10 percent) received two-and-a-half percent of the city's income, and the bottom half received 24 percent. . . . The incidence of poverty in metropolitan Lima (defined as the inability to purchase the basic minimum of food, health, education, housing, and transportation) increased from 30 percent of all households in June 1985 to 47 percent by mid-1988.[68]

The ever-widening gap between the rich and the poor, between the powerful and the powerless, continues to stratify society in Peru.

El Agustino—The Microcosm

All that was happening in Lima starting in the late 1960s was occurring in multiple ways in El Agustino. The internal migration into Lima began after World War II and it increased dramatically in the 1970s and the 1980s. As Manuel M. Marzal, S.J., professor of anthropology at the PUC, indicates:

> El Agustino is a typical barrio of internal immigration that has barely any paved streets. It is a case of the unplanned growth

> of the city; a product of the migratory waves that, since the 1940s, have arrived in Lima searching for better opportunities of life and work. . . . It is not easy to present the modern history of the occupation of El Agustino because of the complexity of factors that should be considered, such as the property owner whose land had been occupied, the types of neighborhood organizations, the legal and political action of the state, the viewpoint of the political parties, etc.[69]

The appropriation of land in El Agustino by the new immigrants presents a paradigm of the struggle of the poor to create a place in which to live. This activity also illustrates the creativity and heroic action of the masses as they organized protest marches, resisted police action to remove them from the land, created systems of protection for their new community, and developed social services to help each other. That they were primarily initiated and led by women is essential to understanding these movements.

However, the chaotic fashion in which the barrio was created has left a legacy of problems. "During the height of the internal immigration," said Modesta Centano Salazar, secretary general of her town council,

> hundreds of people daily would descend upon empty land, often arriving at night to be settled in when the police or military forces inevitably arrived. Roads were created in and around the shanties that the people hastily built, and these haphazard byways became the permanent streets. Electrical lines were strung perilously from existing sources, sometimes miles away. Rain, as thankfully infrequent as it is in this coastal desert climate, created mass disorder as mud flowed in and out of people's homes.[70]

The threats to their lives and the economic chaos that they fled were matched by the subhuman conditions in which they were forced to live in their new homes.

El Agustino exists as a residential area with very little industrial activity and no agriculture. The 1993 census reports that the district had 154,028 inhabitants (76,048 women and 77,980 men).[71] José María García, an economist at the PUC, ranked El Agustino as the second poorest barrio of Lima, second only to the very rural district of Comas.[72] The population density is estimated at approximately 150 people per acre, most of whom live in single-story buildings, many of which are perched on steep hills. Nearly two thirds of the population of El Agustino is employed in the informal sector, employment that hardly ever allows one to reach beyond the poverty level.

The Situation of the Family

The effort merely to survive literally tears families apart. Although no statistics track the number of families that break up so that members can find employment, conversations with El Agustino residents indicate that the separation of family members was common by the 1980s. This often means that a father is forced to live apart and has little contact with his wife and children. With the economy in such poor condition throughout Peru for the past three decades, a father's job away from the family does not ensure decent living conditions for the family. Consequently, the mother, who is more often than not the one who remains with the children in Lima, is forced to struggle for survival on her own. This often requires that she take a low-paying job that also separates her from her children for most of the day. The extended family system that is at the root of familial relations in Latin America also is torn asunder. Grandparents, aunts, and uncles, who normally would step in to substitute for the absent parents, are frequently not living in the same city or province.

The predicament of the family in El Agustino is further challenged by adverse social factors. In addition to a dearth of basic services that are necessary after displacement, literacy is still uncommon for parents,[73] the available employment is usually limited to work as an *ambulante* (itinerant street merchant) or in a low-paying service job, and most family members are forced to seek employment after the age of seven or eight.[74] Infectious diseases, such as tuberculosis, are common and working conditions, largely ignored by government agencies due to lack of resources and the powerlessness of the poor, are often barbaric. There is such a high incidence of violence toward children, adolescents, and women that several organizations have been founded to combat this trend.[75] Posters decrying violence can be seen on the walls of shops, *comedores populares*, restaurants, and churches throughout the barrio.[76]

The Parish of *La Virgen de Nazaret*

Within the boundaries of the parish of *La Virgen de Nazaret* (Virgin of Nazareth) (commonly referred to as El Agustino) are 50 communities, 8 satellite chapels, and 7 ecclesiastical communities serving a population of more than 150,000 people. Each ecclesiastical community contains grassroots organizations that act as outreach for the parish in areas such as catechesis (instruction in the faith), youth groups, juvenile development, adult schools, and human rights commissions. The vast majority of the organizers are women and as the former pastor, José Ignacio Mantecón, S.J. states, "Traditionally, questions of religion, education, health, and development are the issues of the women. Additionally, they are the ones who are the most dedicated. I do not say this to please anyone. It is merely a statement of fact based on my seven years here in the parish."[77]

The parish, founded in 1968, sees its roots in the movements of the church in the last four decades: the promulgations of the Second Vatican Council with their emphasis on social justice; the second *Consejo Episcopal Latino-Americano* at Medellín; and the Thirty-second General Congregation of the Society of Jesus (Jesuits), with its emphasis on "the service of faith and the promotion of justice." As in parishes throughout Latin America, the development of the parish involved a new orientation toward pastoral activity.

Manuel M. Marzal, S.J. describes the evolution of this parish in three steps: first, a brief period of creating a traditional pastoral setting in the *pueblo joven* during the early 1970s; second, a movement toward, and primary emphasis on, social activism on multiple levels in the barrio in the late '70s and early '80s; and third, a healthy synthesis of the pastoral and social thereafter.[78]

In the late '70s, the parish worked with the city and federal governments to develop water, electrical, and drainage services and at the same time initiated educational programs. The goal was to educate a majority of the people about the decision-making processes and to make certain that the projects supported by the government were not merely the dreams of the educated, clerical elite. From this social activist foundation, *Servicios Educativos El Agustino* was born.

Servicios Educativos El Agustino (SEA)

SEA was created in 1978 at the time of government improvements in several districts of El Agustino. Among the improvements was the demolition of unsafe homes in the barrio. However, the funding for the relocation of the families left homeless was not covered. With the economy suffering and the cost of living increasing exponentially, SEA responded to the needs of the people by first creating activist organizations throughout the barrio. As Ofelia Montes López, the director of SEA, explains,

> We work in the medium of accompanying the people in a process of growth. Still, there exists a tension here because, on the one hand, the workers and volunteers at SEA share this common goal of faith doing justice. Sadly, on the other hand, when they go home they are often confronted with a lack of solidarity in their homes and neighborhoods. Slowly, often more slowly than I care to admit, there comes a change. The workers are intimately and passionately involved in working

> toward goals of freedom and basic human rights. We are also seeing the conversion spread. Husbands and brothers and neighbors are listening to us, and a change for the better is taking place.[79]

SEA continued to expand in the intervening years to include the first *Clubes de Madres* (Mothers' Clubs); multiple *comedores populares* (communal dining rooms); *bancos comunales* (communal banks);[80] *Centros de Educación Ocupacional* (Occupational Education Centers); *Vaso de Leche* (Cup of Milk, an infant nutrition program); *Comités de Salud* (Health Committees); *Organizaciones Vecinales* (Neighborhood Organizations); and *panaderías* (bakeries) and restaurants as income-producing ventures.

Women in Peruvian History

Anthropologist Irene Silverblatt indicates that the ancient Andean societies valued women and men equally but almost as separate species, "as if the world were divided into two interdependent spheres of gender."[81] The rise of the Inca state in the fifteenth century resulted in the concurrent rise in male power that was eventually consolidated under Spanish rule. Nevertheless, the female images of earthly regeneration found in *Pachamama* (Mother Earth) live on in contemporary Christian celebrations. Due to the internal immigration of recent years, one finds in El Agustino and elsewhere an amalgam of customs and traditions from throughout the country. However, the identification of many of these customs and traditions in contemporary El Agustino is complicated by their mixture and by some eradication in the process of coming together in a new environment.

Studies have indicated that women were active in the fight against the Spanish invaders in the nineteenth century, although it is usually the male leaders who are remembered.[82] Women were also responsible for maintaining community and family life in this period and the same may be said of women in contemporary Peru.

In 1876, a group of women in Lima opened an *espacio social* (social space) under the direction of Peruvian Sra. Juana Manuela Gorriti. This is the first documented case of women gathering to discuss the future of the country and their involvement in this process.[83] Thirty-two years later, women were admitted to universities in Peru. In 1911, Sra. María Jesús Alvarado Rivera, an organizer in Lima, initiated the first modern, political expression of a women's movement in Peru when she organized a conference entitled *El Feminismo* (Feminism). One of the central demands of the conference was suffrage for all women yet this would take more than four more decades to become law.

Most of the written history of women in Peru focuses on the story of the middle- and upper-class women.[84] This is another indication of the perceived "invisibility" of the poor. Nevertheless, with the rise of the socialist and APRA parties, lower-class women enjoyed a limited degree of involvement. Poor women were invited into the political process due to the attention paid to their plight and to the recognition of the contribution they could make in election successes. Yet it was not until the 1950s that poor women began to come to the forefront of the struggle for human rights and for the rights of women in particular. As Ofelia Montes López said:

> When poor women began to concentrate in urban areas, they were able to share their common experiences and join together to look for solutions to the problems. Before many of these women arrived in Lima, they were often isolated and unable to understand both the immensity of the problems as well as the commonality. The urban experience was frightening but it also meant that they were speaking daily with multiple women, a situation that was probably unusual in the country.[85]

Prior to the move to the city, the family often constituted the unit of production, be it farming, light industry, or small business. The urban environment, however, created entirely new situations that quickly redefined the roles of women. In addition to being the one who was primarily responsible for holding together the fabric of the family, the urban mother was required to enter the workforce to survive. The skills that these women brought with them from the countryside proved to be insufficient in the city. Women and men often were forced into unskilled labor in exploitative conditions, but the women's wages were always subordinated to that of men.

Out of the urban environment and all of the struggles to survive arose the women's recognition that they were the ones who would make a change for the better. They could not afford to remain home to take care of their families, and they began to grow in awareness of their ability to institute improvements. "The growth of women's political consciousness in the cities can be understood primarily as a reaction to the ineffectiveness of male political leadership in addressing the problems of workplace and community felt most acutely by women."[86]

One watershed event was the Mother's Day Protest of May 1980. Newly elected president Fernando Belaúnde Terry had sent his wife into the *pueblos jóvenes* to promote the idea of women making more sacrifices for the sake of their families. This did not sit well with the majority of women, who were already sacrificing as much as they could and still seeing their children die from malnutrition and disease. The Mother's Day Protest was spearheaded by the *Federación Departamental de Pueblos Jóvenes y Urbanizaciones Populares* (Federation of Young Towns and Popular Urbanizations or FEDEPJUP), which united popular organizations in *pueblos jóvenes* throughout the city. For the first time in the history of Lima, women from all social and economic sectors joined together to protest the exploitation they experience. While the results of the protest were many (e.g., price controls on basic foodstuffs, health care initiatives, and legislative action against violence toward women and children) perhaps the most prominent outcome was the indelible image of poor women throughout the city acting as a unified force. As Rosa Canto Castro said, "We felt that we could go forward from that point on."[87]

Machismo

> *Look, it is nothing new that men find us inferior. I saw this growing up in the attitude of my parents toward my brothers, and my brothers' attitudes toward me. Even then, I asked myself, "This can't be right, can it?" To this day, my brothers and I argue over my work at SEA. They feel that a woman's place is in the home. But even they have begun to change their attitude and two of them even help me every week. They understand, as I have come to understand, that one's happiness does not rest solely at home but involves one's neighbors and community. It took years but they have begun to listen to me. This is God at work. When you try to do good, I guess you will always encounter obstacles but when God is on your side. . . .*
>
> Celia Sánchez Rojas
> Secretary-general of her township

A crucial factor to consider when discussing women in Peru is the presence of machismo attitudes throughout society in Peru, as in all of Latin American society.[88] This insidious cultural phenomenon of male attitudes and behavior toward women is a systemic form of oppression. The literal definition of machismo relates to the attitude of power of men over women. While this explanation is accurate, it does not do justice to the pervasive, complicated, and prevalent way it is manifested in society. It is common to see mothers inculcating machismo attitudes in their sons. At the same time, in a flawed reading of femininity, they teach girls to be passive and to accept a secondary place in relationship to men.

This issue is made all the more complicated by the fact that these attitudes are so deeply embedded in Peruvian culture as to be considered the norm by a large percentage of the population, men and women alike.[89] Additionally, mothers may instill a sense of passivity in their daughters, understanding that such a trait may be necessary for them to survive. "We can verify the oppression of women profoundly and systematically by this simple fact: Women live an experience of injustice merely because they are women,"[90] according to Dra. Carmen Lora, professor of psychological pedagogy at the PUC and editor of the periodical *Páginas* for the *Centro de Estudios y Publicaciones* (Center of Studies and Publications or CEP) at the *Instituto Bartolomé de Las Casas*.

The presence of machismo attitudes creates hurdles and impediments in all areas of a woman's life: equality in family and social relationships, opportunities for livelihood and family planning, and possibilities for vocational training and education. These restrictions have a direct impact upon the women of this study because many of them are the first in their families to pursue any type of work outside of the home. They are going against the societal norm of a mother whose existence is primarily domestic.

Participation in social movements also brings about a change in family life, one that gradually results in the recognition of the contributions of women for the good of society. It is significant that the labor of the women at SEA is not rooted in the goals of financial advancement but rather in the assistance of their neighbors and friends. This, in turn, has involved a change of attitude—indeed, a conversion—on the part of their husbands, fathers, and brothers.

Secular Feminism in Peru

The presence of secular feminism is active and plentiful in the major cities of Peru. Unfortunately, the impact of the research and development at the private and governmental women's organizations is almost limited to the educated, upper classes.

María Emma Mannarelli, Ph.D. at Flora Tristan Peruvian Woman's Center illustrates the development of feminist thinking in Peru:

> I believe that there has always been an underlying sense of traditional feminism in Peru. It has never been a major, radical movement but there is a historical tradition of the participation of women in the public space within the limits of each historical context. For example, Peruvian feminist María Jesús Alvarado created her feminist manifesto in 1911. The *Congreso Nacional de las Mujeres* (National Women's Congress)

participated in the Pan-American Conference of Women in Washington, D.C. in 1916.

There was resurgence in the mid-1970s, but this was a small group at first. However, I must ask myself, "Where is the influence of foreigners?" because much of our funding comes from Europe and the United States.

Two other areas of concern are the question of power and relations with the church. First of all, the women to whom we appeal and with whom we work are almost exclusively middle- and upper-class. The power differential between us and the poor women of the country has not been handled. Second, most of us are practicing Christians, and we work with nuns throughout the city. However, when it comes to questions of sexuality and family planning, there exists a gulf that we have yet to bridge in all cases.[91]

There are two major private feminist research centers in Peru: Flora Tristan and *El Movimiento Manuela Ramos* (Manuela Ramos ["everywoman"] Movement).[92] The connections between the women of El Agustino and these feminist organizations are limited.

The government of former president Fujimori established *El Ministerio de Promoción de la Mujer y del Desarrollo Humano* (The Ministry of Promotion of Women and Human Development or PROMUDEH) in 1995. Superficially, this looks like a positive step and in many ways it is. The ministry includes programs for children, women, general human development, nutrition, family welfare, and food assistance. However, as Rosa Dominga Trapasso, a Maryknoll sister, resident of Peru since 1954, and highly regarded and trusted social activist says:

The former minister, Sra. Miriam Schenone, was someone who has never been in close contact with those of us who work for the rights of women. However, the manner in which the ministry was established left her little influence or authority. Her primary function was to distribute food. But do we not already have very organized *comedores* to do this? It would appear typical that she, the only woman in the president's cabinet, would be viewed almost exclusively in the one traditional role of women—the buyer and preparer of food.

Nevertheless, this ministry has given more visibility and more space to the plight of women in Peru. Domestic violence is discussed more openly than ever before and this is the first step in eliminating this heinous problem.[93]

Conclusion

This survey of the context out of which the women of El Agustino emerge and in which they live is necessary in order to understand the elaboration of a theology. In the case of El Agustino, the evolution of the environment in which the women of this study live requires cultural, religious, and political analysis. In the drastically new urban milieu, with terrorism, unemployment, hunger, and homelessness a constant threat, these women are called to extraordinary efforts to survive. Their responses to these challenges—challenges that are a product of the context—necessitate their emergence into the public sphere as well as the awareness of their influence and ability to implement change. Even those phenomena that appear larger than life—machismo attitudes, the downfall of socialism, and globalization—must be encountered. Through their responses to these changes, responses in some ways forced upon them, their insights, and evaluations produce new ways of thinking, acting, and understanding.

The interplay between Christian tradition and human experience is a fundamental part of all theological enterprises. In the case of the women of El Agustino, this demands a rethinking of the classical theological categories. As activist Benedicta "Beni" Serrano Agüero points out, "The traditional ways in which the theologians of the church think are not necessarily the categories through which we understand our God. Does that make our thinking inappropriate? I do not think so. Perhaps the time has come for all of us to think in a different way."[94]

The faith of the women of El Agustino that develops out of their lived experience—the suffering, anxiety, and desolation as well as the joy, hope, and vision of a better future—places them in the role of theologian. The interaction between the theologians of the commonplace and the theologians of the academy will nurture the deepening and broadening of the faith of all involved.

(l-r) Margarita Córdova, head of economic programs, Ofelia Montes López, director, and Carmen Sánchez, coordinator of communal banks, in front of SEA offices in El Agustino

CHAPTER 3

The Women of El Agustino

A Personal Look at the Women

> *In the beginning, I wasn't anyone. I was an average, normal person. With much effort I'm able to do the work that I'm responsible for today. My main challenge has been reading and writing because I left school after the fifth grade. My faith, sense of solidarity, and the desire to help other[s] has served me greatly, despite the fact that I wasn't educated. Before, I didn't give much importance to my faith or spiritual support from the church. But now I understand that without this work, the work of God, we wouldn't be able to have a good foundation as human beings.*
>
> *Martha Vera Belleza*
> General Manager
> *Panadería La Virgen de Nazaret*

In their lives, work, words, and faith, the women of El Agustino reveal the dialectic between God's salvific covenant and the necessity of human effort to work toward this promise. There exists no sense of merely waiting patiently for God to improve miraculously (or otherwise) their human state of affairs. Rather, they demonstrate a deep, abiding sense of their partnership with God. They have committed themselves to be agents of change—agents of their own change—which necessitates stepping into unconventional roles often frowned upon by the government and by the church. They tackle their tasks with courage, fortitude, and perseverance. In the process, they experience profound growth in their faith and support for their work.

These women challenge the role of men in their lives, the ineptitude of government agencies, and the policies of their church. Their work for the good of God's people emanates from their reflections on the word of God and their response to God's call. Repeatedly I heard the women speak of *la llamada de Dios* (the call of God) as something that is not only anticipated but as urgent a response as the need to breathe or eat. These are not pious responses enshrouded in devout language. Rather they are practical reflections born of this historical moment—a moment when they answer the problems of the day as they struggle to build the reign of God in their own context. What is witnessed and heard is realism combined with hope—the women's cognizance of their many and great needs that are sustained by the realization that God is on their side and promises to complete the work already begun.

The women's commitment *to the poor by the poor* provides a paradigm of communitarian culture that contrasts with the individualistic culture so valued in the United States and Europe, a phenomenon that has made itself felt in Peru. Essential to understanding this new paradigm is the fact that these women are Christians responding to Gospel values. Without the benefits (or restrictions) of a formal theological education, they succeed in providing sophisticated theological analysis of their social context and God's presence therein. As they think out their faith in these particular historical circumstances, they pose the questions of a people who have not been previously heard. Their reflections are intertwined with the manner in which the word of God is proclaimed and lived in their community.

Gloria Bravo Palomeque, sales coordinator for the SEA bakery, recalled a homilist who quoted the admonition of Thomas Aquinas that we know more *about what God is not* than what God is. She expanded upon this by stating, "we know that God is not poverty or oppression, hunger or homelessness. But we do learn a lot about God when we respond to what God is not."[1] In this response lies a succinct example of the El Agustino women's understanding of God's plan for humanity, their reflection on God, and the role God calls them to fulfill.

Sra. Bravo, like many others, also embodies in her personal life the understanding that this participation in SEA—participation that is her response to the call of God—in no way leads to any erroneous hope of self-realization. Her participation in charitable work began in 1970 when she was the volunteer treasurer for a neighborhood organization. She began assisting in a *comedor popular* (communal dining room) in 1979 and participated in the founding of the *panadería* as an income-producing function of SEA in 1989. Today, with the skills she acquired from her volunteer and paid work, she could easily move on to a higher-paying job outside of the barrio. However, as she says, "I think that I can participate and assist in the work of God, most importantly collaborating with and helping my people as we search for the solutions to problems."[2] This sentiment may be heard repeatedly among the women.

The faith of the women is the foundation for their courage to be the Christians they are. As Ofelia Montes López, says:

> At times, I feel that my work is daunting; I read and I have my reflections and then I open my Bible and I encounter there *what is so dark and obscure*. This gives me my source of peace, my tranquility. Always I try to live accompanied by those persons here at SEA who have died. Then I feel their companionship and I say, "I can walk; I have this life and the Lord gives me the opportunity to walk with those people who have such overwhelming difficulties."[3] (Emphasis added.)

The language that allows the women to speak about God is rooted in the word of God, their faith, and the experiences into which their faith leads them. Speaking of God comes without restraint, yet responding to God's call is never without a struggle. In fact, the concept of *la lucha* (the struggle) pervades much about which the women speak as illustrated by the words of Irene Cáceres Sánchez, who founded the first *comedor popular* in El Agustino: "If there is some sign of the cross, you know you are on the right path."[4] The struggle is fearful but the fear is never paralyzing.

The women of this study, even if their income has risen, still exist close to the poverty level. They have consciously decided to remain in El Agustino, one of the poorest barrios in Lima. Their perspective of the poor, thus, is twofold: it arises from their personal experience and from their encountering daily the ravages of poverty in the people they are assisting. This is the option *of* and *for* the poor.

A Novel Quality

During the last century, theologians in the Northern Hemisphere wrestled with the problem of the unbeliever and what some label the *post-Christian era*. Also, there has been an increase in the number of situations in which faith is sustained by truisms, dogmatic certainty, and a reluctance to become intellectually involved in the faith journey.

The perceived burden of discipleship—the confusion or frustration that may accompany careful thought about one's faith—results in some leaving the church for less demanding environments. The test of faith and its potential for personal growth is neglected and a comfort zone is sought by some. In other words, the dynamism of a faith-filled life is abandoned for the ease of that which assuages but never challenges.

The women of El Agustino neither desire this path nor have the luxury of even considering it. It is here that we witness a faith brimming with careful thought and reflection. We see not a flight from the church that challenges but a turning to theological reflection and to the teachings of the church in order to meet said challenges. In addition, it is this fresh approach, this newness, which opens a window into which we may observe their local theology.

Brazilian theologian María Clara Bingemer, in her essay "Women in the Future of the Theology of Liberation," wrote:

> Women are active producers of theology, just as they are an object of theological reflection. They bring their own method and a particular perspective with which to conceive and express the traditional topics of the faith within the process of Latin American liberation. . . . From their long experience of silence, women have acquired the wisdom, ancient and always new, that speaks the word and silence, in a harmonious combination of gestures, prophecies, lamentations, and counsels, able to express—though never exhaust—the mystery of the presence of the divine in the human. . . . For a woman, bringing into being theology is like bringing into being a life, a new creature. . . . (The women) are eager to rewrite history from their own point of view, to reinterpret the liberating message of God's covenant with the people and Jesus Christ's liberating act in terms of their own situation of captivity, in order to turn them into a source of strength, insight, and strategy to live and suffer in their struggle.[5]

In this newness we discover that which may be lacking in the examination of faith in other socioeconomic settings. The good news of Jesus Christ must exist contemporarily and it is here that we discover a new genus of intellectual depth—a depth that has been overlooked as a result of the intellectual elitism on the part of some trained theologians.

In the endeavors of the women in this study, we discover in their struggles the promise of faith renewal at the advent of the third millennium. Here is where we may hear the women issuing a call to embrace the world passionately. It is the faith of these women, true yet challenging to tradition, to which we turn. In the process of thinking out their faith in refreshing and different ways—that is, in their way of *doing* theology—the women create an environment in which the examination of their *sitz-im-leben* allows for self-discovery and concurrently compels others—the "outsiders"—to do the same. They speak in new ways of the wisdom and truths of the ages. It is a gift—and a challenge. As Edelmira Aclari Castellares, secretary of a neighborhood school, said,

> It would certainly be possible to look at everything that goes on in El Agustino and think that it was just problems that can never be solved. Instead, our involvement in the community makes us understand that the solutions to the problems touch many areas: our wisdom, faith, and prayer, the participation of people in the barrio, the mayor, the church, the state. I never realized before that the work of God touches every level and demands that everyone be involved.[6]

Voice and Listening in Theological Discourse

From the 1960s on, there was an immense increase in women's engagement in all levels of Latin America society. Increasingly large numbers of Catholic women are struggling to make certain that their church is a church of the poor—that is, a church for the majority of each country's inhabitants. The voices of the women of Latin America play a constitutive role in declaring what the church needs to hear.

After the first meeting that brought women of various Christian denominations together in Mexico City in 1979,[7] women theologians were actively encouraged to participate in the arena of theological interpretation from a woman's viewpoint. However, the women who attended this and subsequent meetings are not all theologians. These conferences encouraged women on many levels to reflect theologically. The fruit of their reflection continues to filter through community organizations operated by women.

The women theologians did not initially develop their own methodology but used that of liberation theologians—starting with an option for the poor and engagement in the praxis of liberation. Eventually, these trained theologians began to shift their focus specifically to an option for poor women.[8] Thus, while the concept of women doing theology in Latin America is hardly novel, the production of theology by Peruvian women has been limited. The theology produced by women about women is limited in Peru to the occasional article in one of the Peruvian theological journals and or a section in a few books.[9] Moreover, exposure is generally limited to a small number of educated people. This situation for theology, then, necessitates searching beyond the customary sources of published books and articles and turning to careful listening.

The concepts of voice, speaking, testimony, narrative, conversation, and enabling are now familiar to us as tools through which we may come to understand better our God, particularly so for women.[10] We are now witnessing the movement from a silent majority[11] to a theological influence.

Women are confronted with such biblical passages as 1 Cor. 14:34 ("Women should keep silent in the churches, for they are not allowed to speak, but should be subordinate, as even the law says.") and 1 Tim. 2:11–14 ("Let a woman learn in silence in full submission. I permit no woman to teach or to have authority over a man; she is to keep silent. For Adam was formed first, then Eve; and Adam was not deceived, but the woman was deceived and became a transgressor."). In addition, they must face the patriarchal traditions of the church that demand the submission and the silence of women. However, women's voices will never be muted again. Notwithstanding, the ecclesiastical environment in which trained, women theologians must function is far from conducive to theological yield. A case in point is the paucity of women theologians acting as *periti* (advisors) to bishops and cardinals worldwide and the absence of even one in Peru.

The presence of women as church is underplayed, if not unquestionably impalpable. Yet there exists in El Agustino a situation, born of necessity, in which women play a prominent role in the parish. José Ignacio Mantecón, S.J., the former pastor of El Agustino, summarized this situation when he said,

> [T]he women are very much in charge. When there is no priest available, which is quite often in a parish with over 150,000 parishioners, she acts as the head: leading Eucharistic services, coordinating all of the groups, motivating the others (most especially the men), visiting the sick, providing counsel—in essence, performing most of the jobs we would ordinarily identify as presbyteral.[12]

This is not to say that the situation is ideal. Patriarchal influences are oblique and insidious. When asked of their concept of the church, the women of SEA customarily mention priests, bishops, cardinals, or the Pope first, although their crucial role in the local church is patently obvious at first observation. When one participates in or views on television the frequent liturgies celebrating feast and holy days, it is strikingly apparent that men control the church. Similarly, the male pronoun is used regularly when referring to God. There is no denying the presence of the "women-as-inferior" thinking of Saints Augustine and Thomas Aquinas handed down through the ages. The Aristotelian archetype of the subordinate human nature of women is transparently present in secular as well as in ecclesiastical society.

Nevertheless, the women of El Agustino are prepared and quite willing to speak to this issue of submission. Each woman's voice breaks the deafening silence of the church. By having the courage to speak, each woman is crying out a fervent "no" to the silence imposed upon her over the centuries. "Women are advancing in many areas and this is good," said Rosa Canto Castro, manager of the SEA restaurant, *La Miel*, "because this shows women's participation in the changes being made. We are advancing, machismo is diminishing, and consciousness-raising is taking place for women as well as men."[13]

This speaking out is an integral part of the conception of a new selfhood—a selfhood bound up in communitarian yearning. This is not merely a creation in the present but it is also a recovery of the past with all that was good *and* bad. As Renny Golden, professor of Women's Studies at Northeastern Illinois University and author of *The Hour of the Poor, The Hour of Women* states:

> The people are no different from people of other cultures, but suffering and a capacity to hope imbue them with a depth that must be experienced to be communicated. . . . It is as ordinary as sacrifice for others, and as inexplicable as the appearance of insurgent hope in those moments when Western psychological development theorists would predict despair or paralyzing grief. It breaks through clouds of passivity and individualism. It is always historically embedded.[14]

Although this was written from Golden's experience of the women in El Salvador, it could equally well describe the women of El Agustino.

With a female consciousness,[15] these women continue to question the societal, economic, and ecclesiastical structures that immure them. They do not question the liberating cry of Jesus Christ but they do unveil enigmas in society, in the church, and in the Bible. These questions particularly arise between their striving for the freedom that Jesus offers and the marginalization that they experience daily. To state it differently, they have come to realize that the point of view of the poor is different from the point of view of poor women. Fr. Gustavo Gutiérrez has summarized this perspective in numerous articles, books, and conversations, and has described poor women as "doubly oppressed, doubly marginalized."[16]

For a myriad of reasons, this problem of peripheral existence is perplexing and difficult to solve. In addition to the inherent machismo attitudes, there exists the age-old patriarchal bearing of the church. While not as apparent as in the past, patriarchy remains a force with which to reckon. Yet, some of this problem is overcome with a degree of common sense and perseverance. When asked about machismo and patriarchal attitudes, Celia Sánchez Rojas, the secretary-general of her township, responded:

> Regarding the church, I think many women get angry because they feel excluded. But you know what? For me, the church is not at the *Plaza Mayor* (site of the Cathedral of Lima) or in the Archbishop's palace or even in Rome with the Holy Father. The church is right here in El Agustino and ever since I gained more confidence through my work, I have never felt that the church turns its back on me. Many times, I have had obstacles in my path but with faith and hard work, I have been able to throw them aside and continue ahead.[17]

Regrettably, to speak or write about the women in this study means examining dehumanizing suffering and abuse. The social consequences of the often-dreadful circumstances in the barrio may appear irresolvable. Notwithstanding, through the sharing and support that takes place in meetings, liturgies, conversations, and in the everyday work environment, women uphold one another through guidance, challenges, and love. As Brazilian theologian Ivone Gebara writes:

> There is a way of doing theology that starts with shared experience from oral transmission, from the simple fact of sharing life. I believe this way of doing theology is what is most representative of the popular milieus. Many women are especially gifted with a deep intuition about human life and are able to counsel, to intuit problems, to express them, to give support, to propose solutions, and to confirm the faith of many people. . . . Some of the women are illiterate. That would pose problems for a more academic doing of theology, but it does not hinder the exercise of ministry. This activity is sapiential; it springs from life, and (life) is its reference point. It is received from God and handed on as a gift.[18]

Some of the gifts that the women of El Agustino pass on are ascertained through their words. Yet the words remain just that unless we listen carefully.

Theology or Vocation?

An apparent and fundamental inquiry at this juncture would be, "What is it that differentiates the local theology that emerges from the faith, words, and work of the women of El Agustino from the life experience of one who lives out her Christian vocation?"

To summarize, it is imperative to recognize that all theologies—especially those that were considered "pure theology" or contextually neutral—are indeed local. Yet the local context from which these "pure" theologies emerged was never acknowledged. Their de facto contextuality was disguised under the umbrella of universality. This denial vitiates the indispensable need for continual engagement with the Gospel of Jesus Christ.

Conversely, the theologies appearing in the last three decades forthrightly assert their local nature. In other words, there is a frank engagement of the conditions and circumstances from which theology emerges. This necessarily involves an in-depth encounter with the goals and aspirations, dilemmas and obstacles, and doubts and apprehensions of the community of faith, as well as the history inherent in any specific context. For instance, one may easily discern from the women's words a leitmotiv of struggle combined with hope for the future. This must not be ignored or underplayed if one is to execute earnestly theological analysis. The context is the lens through which all aspects of theology—spirituality, ethics, Christology, pastoral activity, and so forth—must be viewed and developed. The context is that place in which the religious dimensions of the women's lives exist and through which they—and we—come to understand their theology.

Not to acknowledge and utilize the contexts thus implies that it is possible for dogmatic deduction to unfold beyond human existence. The use of the contextual lens, of course, presents a formidable challenge to the idea that what was brought from Europe in the sixteenth century was all we need to know and understand about salvation. If we are to accept the fact that theologies are not *timeless* in every sense of the word, we must also acknowledge that this cries out for the understanding of the specific time and place.

The skills required for such investigation do not inevitably demand the education that the First World might view as a prerequisite. The wisdom and life experiences, as well as the deeply rooted Christian faith, of these women prepare them superbly for the task at hand. "We have faced huge problems and we have made mistakes," said Zenaida Zúñiga Medina, board member of the Central Federation of *Comedores Populares* of Lima and Callao.

> However, when we *compañeras* come together, even when we want to throw in the towel, we understand that all of the trouble we face personally and professionally prepares us well to move ahead. This means that we find strength to work to promote dignity, for children to have bread, for people to have jobs. We don't have riches but God has given us our hands

> and our eyes to see and with these we can serve the people who need us most."[19]

The community of faith in El Agustino is blessed to have accomplished, thoughtful, intuitive women to guide their theological venture. With the guidance of the women, the journey to discover truth forges on, not with any sense of an absolute and final alighting but with a desire to come to a more complete comprehension of the truth at this time and place.

The women, themselves, clearly attest that they use what theologians call a "hermeneutics of suspicion" concerning proclamations that claim absolutism or independence of context. Lucy Mejia Calderón, coordinator of comedores, clearly indicated this when she spoke of the evangelical denominations in El Agustino and her encounter with one priest:

> Some of my neighbors have begun to worship at the *Iglesia de Cristo* (Church of Christ) in our neighborhood. When I asked them why they were doing this after years of worshiping at (*La Virgen de Nazaret*), they told me that the church makes them feel good and gives them answers. I am happy for them but I wonder if the real reason that they changed denominations is that our parish makes you think about the answers. They are not just handed to you on a plate. The problem I have with the evangelicals is that they seem to have *all* of the answers. Does any human or church have *all* of the answers? (Emphasis added.)
>
> I have had my own encounters with the evangelicals. They want us to change our opinions. They confront us on why we worship these images like San Martín de Porres (a Peruvian saint). I tell them, "I do not worship this piece of concrete, but what the person is and represents for us." There is a sense of history in the Catholic church that I really appreciate. A person needs to be very well prepared in these encounters.
>
> I argued once with a priest because he told me, "I do not see you at Mass on Sundays." I responded, "It's true. I do not come to Mass on Sundays and I will not because Sundays for me are exclusively for the family. It is the only day that my husband and I are home all day and we spend time with our children and talk a lot. I don't believe God is going to stop loving me because I stay at home with my family." I go to chapel and pray all of the time and my family goes to Mass every week—just not on Sundays. And I find God all over, not just in church on Sunday.[20]

Sra. Mejia observes the spirit, if not the letter, of the law and there is no denying her faith and her dedication to the people whom she serves. She also exhibits independent thinking and a practicality that is representative of most of the women of SEA. The search for truth undertakes a distinctly contemporary, necessarily circumstantial methodology that neither ignores the articulations of the past nor ascribes to them superiority.

An examination of the words of the women leaders of El Agustino characterizes the quintessential imperative that any theology, no matter what else its outcome may be, must first of all enable the community to work toward the freedom that Jesus Christ offers. Accordingly, a theology cannot exist solely within the realm of words just as actions themselves are never a theology. This is illustrated by Elvira Torres Anas, coordinator of the *Centro Nacional de Organizaciones Sociales de Base* (National Center of Base Social Organizations):

> My motivation for participating in various organizations like *Vaso de Leche* [Glass of Milk (Children's Food Program)] and *Club de Madres* [Mothers' Clubs] is connected in every way with God and my interpretation of the call of God through my ongoing participation in the Christian communities. I did not always understand at first what I was getting myself involved in. But as time went on, I grew in my understanding of how the Word of God not only calls us to reflect on the Word in our lives but it is also a call to action—a call to act in the cause of freedom.
>
> In this fashion, all of the organizations in which I have been involved are connected to our communal reflection. Our contemplation teaches us and uplifts us when the situation is difficult. The work and the contemplation go hand-in-hand. In this way, we can really make a difference in the lives of the people of our community. This is how I experience God here in the barrio.[21]

Sra. Torres's words illustrate how the theology of these women—that is, the product of their communal reflection—provides a deeper understanding of their faith, a call to action, a constantly evolving understanding of this call, support for the troublesome times, and an answer to the question of the incarnation in the here and now. Is this not what any theology should do?

This is not to say that all that emerges from the faithful may be called a "theology." Nevertheless, to those who are called "professional theologians," it is a compelling reminder of the absolute necessity of remaining in close contact with their community, wherever or whatever it may be.

Theology emerges concretely from people in community such as Sra. Torres—those who continually act, reflect on their actions, come to a more complete understanding of the complex relationship between the two, and possess the ability to verbalize on the actualization of their goals. Their questions and endeavors provide the foundation for a lived faith and it is their constantly evolving answers that are veritable proofs of a theology—a faith seeking understanding.

From the women's words and actions come the theological character and the insightful understanding of their theology. Here we see their acumen as it is applied to an ever-growing set of concrete situations: protection and preservation of life; personal development in the areas of spirituality, work, and family life; a call to an ever-increasing understanding of their faith; a faithfulness to the experience of their community, society, and the traditions of their church; increasing love of God; the efficacy of God in their lives; and the understanding of God's love for them.

The word of God, a sense of the presence of God, an understanding of their community, and the subsequent responses, answer the question of the role of the community in the creation of a theology.

The Local Church

The emphasis on the universality of the church, markedly present in the papacy of John Paul II, presents possible difficulties in understanding how the local church and the universal church exist together and relate to each other. The role of the magisterium and the Pope was exemplified by John Paul II. He writes:

> Obviously (the Second Vatican Council in *Lumen Gentium* 25, or *The Light of Humanity*, the Dogmatic Constitution of the Church) specifies that an essential condition for the value and obligatory quality of the bishops' teaching is that they are in communion with the Roman Pontiff and speak as such. Certainly each bishop has his own personality and presents the Lord's teaching by using the talents at his disposal. But precisely because it is a question of preaching the Lord's teaching entrusted to the Church, he must always remain in communion of mind and heart with the visible head of the Church.[22]

In John Paul II's 1995 encyclical on the reunification of the Christian churches, *Ut unum sint* (That All May Be One), he wrote:

> When circumstances require it, (the Pope) speaks in the name of all the pastors in communion with him. He can also—under very specific conditions clearly laid down by the First Vatican Council—declare *ex cathedra* that a certain doctrine belongs to the deposit of faith. By thus bearing witness to the truth, he serves unity.[23]

These statements, in and of themselves, would appear to be acceptable to the women of El Agustino (and to many others) although it must be noted that the implicit authorities are all male. An insight into the particulars—here, the possible, intrinsic discord between the local and the universal church—is suggested clearly by the words of one of the women. While not speaking of *Lumen Gentium* or *Ut unum sint*, Sra. Montes López raises a challenging question in relation to those texts:

> What would the cardinal (of Lima) or the Pope think if he knew that we (women) assume many priestly roles here in the parish? We do this because it is necessary. We do this in response to the call of God. We do *not* do this because we are angry women challenging the church with no regard for church teaching. Should we feel that our call is not legitimate?[24] (Emphasis added.)

Theologian Sally M. Vance-Trembath, in her insightful analysis of *Ut unum sint*, and with an invitation reminiscent of the pragmatism of the women of El Agustino, approaches the problem from a different angle. She writes:

> One of the ways we come to conversion is by noticing inconsistency. Recognizing a lack of coherence is often the first step toward change. Authority figures in particular ought not to be inconsistent lest they lose their power to guide. If this is the case with secular authorities, it is all the more so in the Church, which seeks to guide humanity in its activities for the sake of the historic mission of Jesus Christ. The leadership in the Church has treated two alienated groups inconsistently: the separated Christian churches (that is, the focus of the encyclical, *Ut unum sint*) and women members of the Catholic Church. In different ways and at different times in its history, the Church has said to these two groups, "you fall short."
>
> . . . When the pope invites the separated Christians into this expanded dialogue (amongst Christian churches), he emphasizes the need for conversion on the part of both dialogue

> partners. . . . So the first principle (of repentance), that calls for a recognition of harm done, cannot be addressed unless the very anthropology that impugns women's participation in the work of the Gospel is also addressed. . . . When the church takes the same steps (of reconciliation) with women as it has done with other Christians, it will be taking one of its own success stories as a model and solving one of its own most destructive pathologies at the same time.[25]

Thus, the question of the relationship between the universal and the local church remains a problem. The universal church would seem to be upholding uncritically much of what has existed throughout the ages.

The women in this study, on the other hand, can be very precise about what it is that they need from the church in order to facilitate their survival in an often adversarial world. These women continue to expose the unsympathetic, nonliberative, autocratic, dogmatic approaches of their church and slowly chip away at them in order to infuse their church with a spirit more consistent with the Gospel of Jesus Christ. Through this process, they are creating their own identity in which the probability of immuring is greatly lessened. They believe that the church brought to them by the Spaniards most certainly contains the truth—*but not the entirety of the truth*. They understand that the latter is something for which each age must struggle. "I can really say that my faith is completely different, larger and more alive, than before I started to work at SEA," said Irene Cáceres Sánchez. "Before I would blame God. I thought that since God knew the situation, he should fix it. I would leave everything for God to do. Now we know that we are the ones who need to do what is necessary, what God wants, which is to have life with dignity, to be governed with justice. These were not the ideas I was taught in church when I was young."[26]

Dignity and justice were not always goals for which the women set out to achieve. Rather, the foremost objective was the preservation of life in their environment. Yet, as they labored in this regard, the horizons became rich with other fruits: a deeper understanding of their faith; a realization that their individual suppositions were shared by many; a confirmation of God's presence; assurance that they could achieve a yielding of results in their own fashion; and a building of confidence to move ahead. This encapsulates the local church in the barrio of El Agustino. It may not always live in harmony with the universal church but, because of this, it presents important challenges to the contemporary church—for example, the role of women, the sources of theological thought, the need for all believers to live in an atmosphere in which they may actively think out their faith, as well as the integral component of social activism in the teaching of Jesus Christ.

Faith Lived Out Loud

> *Last week there was a meeting where a woman came with a one-year-old baby with a cerebral hemorrhage. She is desperate because the hospital is demanding money or food for payment. She doesn't have either. I told her to go to SEA and speak with the social worker. But some of the people in the* comedor *were upset because they didn't want her to have more than her share of the food. I asked them, "Why was the* comedor *established?" All of us need to put something in to cover this expense even if it means adding a bit of water to the soup in order to help this lady.*
>
> Gloria Bravo Palomeque

There is a fundamental recognition of the presence of sin in the lives of the women of El Agustino. This is experienced in many forms: personal, communitarian, societal, and ecclesiastical. With this identification of wrongdoing and systemic inequities comes a refreshingly honest approach to life together with faith. While accepting themselves as corpus Christi, they are fully cognizant of the dialectical character of sin and human nature and speak of it candidly.

The antithesis of all that is good is readily found outside of one's door—and oftentimes behind it too. The "good" stands out even more distinctly—the good toward which they strive. We observe in their midst an understanding of both the sanctity of their Christian community and their lives, as well as the ardently negative influences that are divisive and diminish the feasibility of dignity and justice. These conditions do not allow them to indulge in some romanticized image of community or church. In their reflections on Scripture and life, they have come to understand that to be a Christian and to live in a Christian community never guarantees an absence of conflict. This is more than obvious in the words of Carmen Fernández Cano, a community organizer in El Agustino:

> We come together each with our own gifts and our own opinions. It is no secret that when you get any group of people together there will always be disagreements and arguments. But God has put us here with just these gifts so that we can work together and not against one another in the building of the kingdom. St. Paul writes of this in his letter to the Corinthians. (1 Cor. 12) But the Holy Spirit gives us these gifts so freely and it is up to us to put the pieces together into the body of Christ.
>
> I especially relate to the verse when St. Paul says that no part of the body of Christ is any less important or honorable

> than another. If you were to put me and my neighbors up against some people from Miraflores (a wealthy neighborhood of Lima), I doubt that your average person would say that we were just as important or worthy. But God is there saying just that: We are![27]

True community requires in-depth knowledge of all that affects it and this foreordains an appreciation of the gifts each person possesses, an admission of what hampers progress, and an awareness of the cultures that interact therein. This inescapably affords the possibility of seeing and recognizing things we may prefer to hide. But this is the sine qua non of living your faith "out loud." The women of this study have woven this process into all that they do. They accomplish the thinking out of their faith in a variety of ways. As they tackle increasingly complex concerns, they also progressively clarify the relationships that tie them together.

The Theological Context of El Agustino

Poverty is the primary factor influencing life in this barrio. The question of daily survival is omnipresent and occupies the activity of most residents. This establishes an undeniable boundary between the people here and the wealthier citizens of their own city. In every sense of the word, this is the *Third World.* First and foremost, poverty is the context in which all theological reflection must take place.

La Llamada de Dios

The oft-mentioned *llamada de Dios*, or "call of God" to which the women of El Agustino respond must be carefully defined. Herein we find an elemental aspect of their search for truth and liberty in their world. In that sense, the call of God is indispensable both as a demand and as a step toward a deeper understanding of God. There also exists the realization that each generation of believers (as well as each individual believer) takes part in rediscovering the truth that is universal and particular to each context.

Modesta Centano Salazar, secretary general for her town council and coordinator of the *Movimiento de Trabajadores Cristianos* (Christian Workers Movement), explained their commitment in this fashion:

> SEA and the Christian communities give us the opportunity to reflect and to be formed. And this is not just for the leaders but also for all the people. Yet, we realize that we will always be challenged—challenged to know what we are talking

> about, to constantly turn to the Bible for inspiration, to question our preconceptions, to listen to differing opinions, to change our minds.
>
> At times, I can feel overwhelmed by the complexity of the problems and by the teachings of the church. But this is never a reason to stop thinking and learning and growing. I think of Jesus at those times and I know that the path he was on all the way to the cross was not always easy. But I also think that Jesus' path was filled with joy, contentment, and moments of peace. And so is mine. In that way, I truly feel I am imitating Christ in my life.[28]

For these women, recognizing the call of God entails a search for the summons itself in all that surrounds them. Necessarily, this first means a true sense of belonging to community—the community of their parish, their barrio, their country, the universal church, and humanity. Inasmuch as this entails a concrete acknowledgment of those in their primary environs, the dilemma of poverty rises to the top as a contradiction to Jesus Christ's abundant offer of full life and peace.

Poverty is also that to which they must respond first in their answer to the call of God. Thus, this answer—their action—does not necessarily predestine their wholehearted response to a set of church doctrines but rather their concern for the people of their community. The latter will lead to the affirmation of church dogma if the dogma in question proves to be legitimate in the test of life.

Intrinsically, it is always through action first that they come to understand their God and their church and not from a blind acquiescence to church tenets. Teleologically, the goals may be the same but the path is assertively different. The women acknowledge the fact that their action is only a step in the process of living in community and believing in God. The awareness they achieve and the urging to which they respond as they engage in the real life of their community emerges from an intelligent, candid, and spiritual consideration of their reality, their church, and their God.

"I think the word of God must be present in our daily lives and in every space," said Sra. Torres.

> We need to incorporate this, especially in our work. The feeding of a hungry person could be just that—feeding someone food. But if we take the time to look at the "why," we come to understand that we are all instruments of God. If we help others, it's because God wants it so. Coming to understand this, however, can take some work. It's worth it, though. We then discover how we can be supported for the future. This may

> not always be the first objective of the church but it has to be our first objective when lives depend on us.[29]

This awareness presupposes an understanding of their church and religion that is reflected in their conversations and observations. They exhibit a knowledgeable foundation from which their personal reflections come forth. There is the corresponding knowledge of the faith with the ever-present desire to know and understand more. While some may regard this as a possible avenue to the increase of doubt, they embrace the increase of their own knowledge with a passion reminiscent of their work.

As is obvious from the words of Sra. Centano, and those of others, they do not seek refuge in contemplation. Rather, they pursue a realization of the interrelatedness of their work, understanding, and church. We find no a priori contemplation of Jesus Christ as God but a fuller concept of Christ as deity and human—that is, of Jesus experiencing much of what they themselves experience. The God who is Jesus suffers and the *theologicus crucis* (theology of the cross) is an important hermeneutic for their theology. This engagement between the life they live and the steps they take to understand the call of God provides a refreshing admission of the requisite and intimate relationship of the two.

Interaction with Tradition

> *I approach life with the understanding that there is a great deal I do not know now nor will ever know. But I do know this: all of our ancestors lived their lives gathering wisdom as we do too. So, I look to the Bible and our history for signs of what we should be doing.*
>
> Zenaida Zúñiga Medina
> Board member of *comedores populares*

The women of SEA realize that they are not alone in the activities they pursue. First, there is an understanding that they are trying always to do God's work—that is, the work of which God would approve. Furthermore, they look to the history of their people and Christians everywhere for knowledge. Repeatedly, they turn to the narratives of the Bible and to prayer for assistance in this effort. This provides an assurance that they do not fall into the pattern of spiritualizing matters, a destructive archetype found throughout the history of Christianity. As Martha Vera Belleza, general manager of *La Panadería de La Virgen de Nazaret*, states,

> [I]f I am to call myself a Christian, I strongly believe that this means constant work at understanding what this means. Some

> believe that all they have to do is to be baptized, while others take this one more step and see the necessity of going to Mass on Sunday as a sufficient response. I say that we take one step more—one step at a time in understanding our God. When something bad happens, I do not think that God is happy if I just offer this as a sacrifice and do nothing about it.[30]

Many such scrutinies may be stifled by fear that Christian beliefs will be discovered wanting, but here we find a genuine desire to sustain an examination of the faith. For example, one may not expect to hear discussions in this poor barrio of the humanity of Christ and the solution worked out at the Council of Chalcedon (451 C.E.). Nevertheless, these occur as well as frequent conversations about church history and contemporary church documents. This is not to claim that we are discovering biblical scholars or ecclesiastical historians. Still, both of these groups and other theologians would do well to listen to such conversations.

Very clearly, there is a questioning of traditions—traditions that seem to be incomprehensible or antithetical to the freedom of the Gospel. In particular, the role of women in the church is an ardent concern. They are not willing to accept blindly that which has been passed down through the generations. The delicate balance between life and death that exists in El Agustino does not afford the opportunity to receive much uncritically. While this might appear to be the more comfortable and nonconfrontative path, it is not one that they take. On the other hand, there is no rejection of tradition either. They look here for a confirmation that their faith and their church are constantly evolving. They seek as well a discernment of the history and the immensity of their participation in God's work here on earth. Thus, there is a balance between inappropriate dependence on and a declaration of independence from the rich tradition of the church.

As Relinda Sosa Perez, who is in charge of one of the *comedores populares*, said:

> Does it not seem obvious to you that the exclusion of half of the world's population is not something that God would want? The church exists for us, not us for the church. And if women have absolutely no say in how the church operates, then we exist for the church.
>
> I do believe that the day is coming when we women will play a greater role justified by our being creatures of God and baptized members of Christ's body here on earth. Then, and only then, will the church exist in such a way as to foster the promotion of God's work in the way it is intended it to be.[31]

Conversion and Hope

> *Look, I don't go to church much but I sure like their bread.*
>
> José, a street person in El Agustino

The roles that the women of El Agustino assume go beyond the normal societal and ecclesiastical expectancies. Unquestionably, the tasks that they undertake potentially place them in a conflictual situation with their families, neighbors, community, and the institutional church. Without any doubt, the women themselves, as well as their families and neighbors, are undergoing a continual process of change we will call "conversion." Yet, to what end, one may ask?

As Benedicta "Beni" Serrano Agüero queries, "should we not be concerned that in a country that professes to be 95 percent Christian, there is so much poverty, homelessness, and violence. Are these conditions considered Christian?"[32] In examining her question, we confront the fact that Peruvian Christianity may possibly be viewed as a failure unless we accept a theology of self-mortification. Another way to state the problem is this, How are we to reconcile these failures without slipping into skepticism and doubt?

In a country as culturally Catholic as Peru, it is difficult to accept the inherent social conditions as anything but sinful and shameful, as is the case in every Christian country in the world. What then is the solution? The presence of doubt is assuaged in some cases by the simple fact that, for many Catholics in Peru, faith is more blind than thinking. As elsewhere, a great deal of attention is being paid to the unbeliever or to the "threat" of Protestant denominations. In other words, the greatest problems—that is, those that Sra. Serrano indicated—often take a lesser role in the works of the church and government officials.

The women of SEA take an antipodal stance. The church is alive in El Agustino because it responds to the most basic needs of the people. Even with its failures and inconsistencies at times—or perhaps because of this—it actively works toward solutions without issuing promises of having all of the answers or being able to solve every problem. Secularism is not seen as a threat to the church but a vivid reminder that a community of faith must consistently reevaluate its experience of Gospel values. In this regard, we witness a great deal of effort toward balancing the two constants of which theologian Hans Küng speaks: "the present world of experience in all its ambivalence, contingency and change" and "the Judaeo-Christian tradition which is ultimately based on the Christian message, the Gospel of Jesus Christ."[33] The heart of the matter for the women here is the actualization of efforts on behalf of the people, which encourage the ongoing conversation and understanding of the world and, through the resulting efforts, create an atmosphere in which the church may constantly renew itself.

The hope for the future that sustains their labor is not supported by any triumphalistic vision of their church. Rather, it is deeply rooted in an understanding of the opposite. As María Ramos Vega, a young coordinator of the *Comedor Forjemos Alegría* (Building Happiness Communal Kitchen) whose mother was one of the founding leaders of the *comedores populares* in El Agustino states, "We understand from Jesus himself that the kingdom of God is not of this world. I am not interested in building kingdoms. What I want to do is help the people in my small way here and now."[34] Ofelia Montes López echoed her words when she said,

> I smile when I witness large organizations like governments or oil companies or even the institutional church in trouble. These are all agencies with a great deal of power and money. Their shortcomings are a signal that they have something very serious to look at. I truly believe that the power of, and the preservation of power in, these organizations stands in the way of understanding and hearing the voice of Jesus. As they struggle, it will be easier to hear his voice.[35]

An acceptance of their church as the one that emerges from their actual, experiential situation is illustrated in these words and in their actions. Their church responds to the condition of the community while it simultaneously substantiates the values of the faith community. Admittedly, this negates the possibility of providing comfort or contentment in promises of a better life in the hereafter. Yet, in the course of embracing the vulnerability that each one of God's creatures experiences, the efforts of the women allow the people to imagine concretely a better place.

The unrelenting analysis of the conditions of this world, combined with the undertakings to make a change for the better, yield to a more realistic approach to the human condition. Sra. Bravo summarized this in the following fashion: "We must ask ourselves if a church full of dead and dying people is our goal. I worry about adequate nutrition and housing first and then I can worry if they have been to confession."[36]

The women's tasks and goals are not as easily reached as it may appear. The repudiation of the traditional woman's role comes with serious consequences. The women often speak of disagreements with, and alienation from, husbands, fathers, and neighbors after they went to work at SEA. As Rosa Pacheco, a coordinator of *Federación Popular de Mujeres* (Federation of Women) said:

> I knew from the very beginning that I was taking a risk when I started working with SEA. My husband questioned why I was spending so much time away from home. My daughters, however, put the question more directly. They asked me, "Why?" What I told them then and what I tell them now is the same: there are times in your life when you do things you do not completely understand but it is important sometimes to listen to your heart and not your mind.[37]

Although many of the women moved from volunteer to paid work within the organization, the salaries reflect those of NGOs throughout the world. Economic considerations often added to the complaints the women received. However, with perseverance, changes came about over the years, specifically in five primary ways.

First, their sense of self-esteem and confidence was invariably heightened. Edelmira Aclari Castellares said, "I was scared at first to speak at organizing meetings. I was the only woman among four men. But we have learned to reflect, to correct ourselves, and to accept that we all make mistakes. I know now that we women need to value ourselves. Then we can improve ourselves and accomplish much more for others."[38]

Second, there is a growth in knowledge of their church and a deepening of their faith. The exploration of church history and documents does not result in a rise in doubt; rather an intensification of their commitment. Biblical analysis is the prerequisite for the start and continuation of any project, be it a nutrition program, voters' rights, business start-up, or a housing development. With a consistent reference to biblical stories, the lessons of the Bible are brought alive. Examination of the manner in which the faithful have lived over the centuries, as well as analysis of the formal response of the church, informs the women of possible directions.

Third, these two factors eventually had an influence upon those who previously had doubted or even resented the women's involvement in social action. This impact filtered down to the men in the lives of the women and resulted in active participation on the part of many of the fathers, brothers, husbands, and sons. The women witness and confess the changes that take place with these men. "I do not think that any of us will ever completely understand the presence of love in our lives," said Relinda Sosa Perez, the general manager of one of the *comedores populares*.

> But I know that my husband loves me even though he disagreed at first with my volunteer work. But through his love for me and mine for him and my obvious love for the people for whom I work, he came to understand and appreciate what

> I am doing. I feel that this is the way God's love for all of us grows. It's addictive.[39]

Fourth, the daughters, granddaughters, and nieces of these women were able to see them as models for the manner in which they should live their lives. These young women grew up experiencing women who were public figures in a society where poor women (and women in general) primarily exist in the private domain of the household. The daughters lived with a mother who created a balance of public and domestic tasks that is still rare in all levels of Peruvian society. They began to value from an early age the necessity of knowledge, involvement, and commitment to themselves and to their community.

"I admire my mother a lot for the work that she does," said Esther Arteago Serrano, coordinator of *El Movimiento de Los Niños* (Children's Movement) and daughter of activist Benedicta Serrano.

> She has always been concerned that I am aware of what she does and why she does it. I've learned about her focus and her strength for wanting to do new things to help others. Her work took her out of the house a great deal but I never felt that she was leaving us alone. We would often accompany her to the projects. When she had to be away, she always had a way of letting us know why. I have witnessed how alive she is when she is working for the good of others. It would be hard not to want the same thing—to want to feel that close to God.[40]

Although the involvement of men in social activist and ecclesiastical activities is hardly unknown, it is the commitment of the women in this impoverished barrio that has the greatest impact. María Ramos described this commitment:

> I did not really understand it when I was growing up but even then, I had the feeling that my mother was different from the mothers of my friends. She did not just go to work, then come home, and not talk about what she was doing. She always made sure that we knew what she was doing and why. We understood that she was answering *la llamada de Dios* and what that meant for her.
>
> And it was not just (her children) she spoke to. My father and uncles, the neighbors, and all of the women in the neighborhood heard about the activities of SEA and why they were important. Looking back, I can now say that she almost single-handedly was a deliverer of hope to many of these people.

> When I was little, we did not even have electricity or running water. I remember that after the fight to have these available was won, she said to me, "Look! Did you see how many new people are coming to church and getting involved now? If we do God's work, God will bring the people back.[41]

Underlying this statement is a prayerful admittance of the mystery of life and of God's action in the world. "My decision to get involved with *Vaso de Leche*, my first volunteer group, was difficult because we needed the money and it meant my leaving my job," says Sra. Serrano.

> But I did quit my job and I got involved—and I have never regretted it. Eventually I was elected *Presidenta de la Federación de Comedores Populares de Lima y Callao* (president of the Federation of Communal Dining Rooms of Lima and Callao, the latter being a large port city adjacent to Lima). This was just when the violence was escalating in Peru and I received several death threats from the terrorists. I guess that any sane person would have quit and gone into hiding. So I guess I am saying I am *loca*—crazy for God, if you will. Really deep down I was scared and I was conscious of the danger. But when I would go out, I would commend myself to God and I felt God was carrying me. I would read the Bible beforehand and go with the messages I found there.[42]

An explanation of such self-sacrifice is nearly impossible to present. However, I turn once again to Sra. Serrano, for her words come from the heart of experience:

> Among the poor, we strengthen ourselves and we begin to grow in the light of our faith in Jesus Christ, who became human and poor so that we might be liberated. Many times, we are tied to our fears and we stay that way. But I believe that our reflection in community is a moment of theology when we have the ability to respond. God has given us a liberation of service, sharing, and loving. It is in an option of liberation if I choose life. Then, I must defend life for others whether in the organizations, in my family, or in my Christian life. For me, liberation is a choice, a task, and a gift from God.[43]

Conversion and *hope* are familiar terms in theological studies. Yet, in contemporary Christianity, these cardinal elements of our faith are often underplayed. The women, however, live them out in their animation of the Gospel. Their lives are proof that God does, indeed, have a plan for humanity and they work actively as agents of this plan. The end of humanity for the greater glory of God does not linger in the realm of the academic or spiritual but is concretely, vividly, tangibly visible in what they do. In this style, the women help others to hope again.

This entails not mere certitude in their Christian beliefs but a commitment to the people of God at their neediest. This is a laborious task yet nourished by their faith—a faith that is no stranger to defeat, frustration, and righteous anger. This is a faith, inspirited with wisdom, which is well prepared to deal with such hurdles.

Despite the poverty, the laissez-faire attitudes of their government, life-threatening terrorism, and a multitude of other debilitating plights, they are aware of the dignity of *each* human being.

Although the women seldom speak in the terminology of anthropological theology, their actions explicitly indicate that they consider each human being significant and worthy. It is not difficult to understand, in an environment where hopelessness is commonplace, that their love, care, and attention impart much needed meaning to people's lives. Jesus said, "by their fruit you will recognize them" (Matt. 7:20) and we do, indeed, perceive these women as the bearers of hope. And the hope they instill is not the fruit of world-changing programs but the acts of good Samaritans.

Activities such as assistance in finding a home, or helping to start a business that will provide for a family, do not ordinarily fall under the category of theology. But these acts *are* theologically meaningful because they "choose life, so that you and your children may live" (Deut. 30:19).

Dialogue

A discussion of the importance of dialogue in the development of the theology of the women of SEA presupposes their knowledge of the faith, the richness of their experiences, and the commitment they exhibit. In fact, for these women, the three components are inseparable and lead into a hermeneutical spiral—a spiral that leads them up to the full integration of the faith, experience, and commitment.

The theological experience, in this sense, is partially corporal and encompasses the mind, the soul, *and* the body. In truth, their theology is premised upon the belief that the three coexist. Their dialogical pedagogy is seen in the process of intelligently examining their world, church, and God.

Superficially, it would appear that dialogue is an integral part of their theology—that is, what is described as a thinking faith. What exists among these women is an *intensity* of dialogue. By this, I mean an overriding and natural concern about the particular that leads to a greater comprehension of the more universal. In their examination and living out of the experience of El Agustino, they come closer to the idea of mystery and transcendence.

Each one of the women speaks of how they sense a deepening of their faith through their commitment to the people. Equally so, they confess the surprise brought by this greater understanding of Jesus. "We take the messages of the Bible quite seriously," said Rosa Canto.

> And in the Bible, you do not find just lectures from Jesus or prophets but you discover conversations, too. This world is God's creation and it is here where we will discover God. But this does not happen by magic. It is a process that encourages one to move on to new insights. Look at it this way: when you were a baby, you were talked at. As time goes by, you began to put the words and thoughts together and were able to ask your own questions and make your own statements. But this was not enough. You eventually started to have an exchange of ideas with people. From this, you were able to learn and grow. Well, it is the same with us now. We must talk with one another in order to understand what we are doing, why, and where we discover God here.[44]

The distinction between the divine and the human is lessened in this dialogue. Carmen Fernández explained it in this fashion:

> We read the Bible and it is there that we come to understand that the presence of God was often experienced most intensely when people, for example the Jews, were having the most trouble. With this idea, we then begin to discuss how this might be possible for us in El Agustino. Ultimately we realize that the poverty in which we live actually allows us to see God more clearly. We cannot worry about things that are inconsequential when our neighbor or friend is sick, or dying, or unable to support a family. This understanding does not come just from our private reflection but grows into action as we talk about it.[45]

As Frei Betto (née Carlos Alberto Libanio Christo), a Brazilian theologian and adviser to base communities, wrote:

> The reality (of poor communities) is completely different from the analysis that many make. For example, many believe that the proletariat is waiting for someone to appear, someone

> incorporating its aspirations, and then it will rise up. This is a deception. There is an entire learning process of injection, dialogue, openness, and transformation of consciousness that the proletariat is carrying out and we are not.[46]

The women use their experience of the poverty and all of its ramifications to explore the very personal way in which these affect their lives and how they might see God in these circumstances. These experiences involve both the intensely poignant hands-on sights of humanity struggling for survival as well as the more transcendent analysis of feeling, mood, and consciousness-raising. They engender and advance theological reflections. Just as Jesus was a flesh and blood experience for the people of the first century, he is the same for these women in the people they encounter. "Remember," advises Rosa Pacheco, "Jesus said, 'whatever you do for one of the least of these people of mine, you do for me'" (Matt. 25:40).[47]

Who Are the Poor?—A Different Conception

> *Jesus did not become human* and *rich. He came to us as one who was poor. If this does not prove that God is on our side, what will?*
>
> Edelmira Aclari

As Paulina Flores de Osorio, founder of the town of San Pedro, El Agustino, says:

> I have seen how often the people receive a very traditional catechesis of a distant God, a God of power and might, a God who is the judge. This creates a distance between the people and God. It stirs up their sense of unworthiness. It contributes to their lack of sense of having any control over their life and destiny. This makes their spirits poor and that adds to their already present material poverty. And this is not the God we pray to.[48]

Implicit in Sra. Flores's words is the concept of the nonperson. Essential to our faith is the passion and death, descent into hell, and resurrection of Jesus Christ—in other words, Christ's human ignominy, complete experience of nonbeing in hell, and ultimate triumph over death. As Christ promises, "I tell you the truth, if anyone keeps my word, he will never see death" (John 8:51). However, with the Peruvian church's emphasis on God's complete victory over death, there exists a distancing of the earthly experience of Jesus; a focus away from the actual struggle of the nonperson. Theologically, a God who is distant, judging, and powerful, to use Sra. Flores's words, is far removed from the Jesus whose human existence was an authentic struggle.

The God of the Bible is one who consistently questions and challenges the institutions of power. This theme is forfeited when disproportionate significance is placed on the triumphalistic God in contrast to a divinity that is both awe-full and accessible. Jesus came, and came as poor, so that each one of us might discover the personal way that God loves us.

The women of SEA discover and grow in this love by first loving their neighbors. In this fashion, they discover both the grace and the downfall of power. "When we first started *Vaso de Leche*," said Ofelia Montes López,

> our goal was quite simple. We realized that a cup of milk was all that stood between a child living or dying. So, our mission was to get that cup of milk to the lips of the child. As the program grew in Lima and throughout Peru, it became necessary for us to interact more with the structures within the country that are responsible for distribution and financial support. In this way, we grew to be very familiar with the idea of power and how it can be used for the betterment of humankind. Yet, we also discovered the selfishness, greed, and thoughtlessness that are present wherever power exists. We went from wanting milk to interacting with power structures to coming to a better understanding of the concept of power. The last two were not our original goals but God always has surprises in store.
>
> We are now very careful within SEA to reassess constantly the issue of power, our contact with it, and how we use it. You do not have to look very far outside of our doors to see that power has been used for centuries to oppress the people. We also understand that we must be empowered in many ways in order to make a change for the better. This also means that we must be instruments of empowering others to do the same.[49]

This attentiveness to, and concern about, the question of power comes from those who are "doubly oppressed, doubly marginalized." Power—both interpersonal and systemic—has been used as an instrument of abuse in the lives of each of these women. Nevertheless, the women also speak of the power they possess in giving and promoting life, as mothers and as companions of the poor. An understanding of this type of power necessarily focuses on the power of love, and this may reach into the realm of the ambiguous and incongruent. The reality of the power of love, however, is much too strong and too valuable an element in their lives to ignore, however confusing defining it may be.

Love in El Agustino, and as a foundation for Christian ethics, is fundamental. Through the acknowledging, nurturing, and offering of love, the women give and sustain life in many forms. It calls each one of the women to act on the behalf of the other, sensitively and concretely.

The lives of the people for whom they struggle have been broken by destructive and selfish power structures. Therefore, their task is clear—they must respond to the need for healing by loving the other into being. Where elements of control broke apart lives, they are now spiritually and physically nourished by benevolence and goodwill. This entails destroying the mask of anonymity so prevalent wherever the poor live. The concept of listening, integral to this study, is also a central focus in the manner in which they act. "Remember the story of Zacchaeus?" asked Sra. Torres.

> Well, I think that story tells us two things. First, I hope that each of us is just as eager as Zacchaeus was to see the face of Jesus in everyone we encounter. But I also hope that we are so prepared to hear the words of others that we might even hear the things that are not spoken. This is what Jesus did. Zacchaeus never said a word but Jesus knew what he wanted.[50]

It is also understood that power possesses the ability to corrupt and this is obviously paradoxical to their goals. They do not want to assume characteristics that portray them as "rescuers." Soraya Ronquillo Peña, Ph.D., coordinator of the Women's Team, put it this way:

> Our work in *Equipo Mujer* (Women's Team) has a focus of accompanying women who are able to assume roles in different projects. In order to create a balance these past ten years, we have shaped women with the skills to establish projects in their own neighborhoods. One of our strategies is to identify leaders who have the ability to implement consciousness-raising so that they are able to accompany other women in different projects. Therefore, each time a new project is started, we have fewer SEA staff involved. In this way, the good is self-perpetuating.[51]

The question of dignity is rooted in the actions and policies of SEA and in the motivations of the women. The issue of poverty is hardly limited to the presence or absence of material goods or the resources to obtain them. Injustice, alienation, and exploitation are primary contributors to the reality of being poor.

As early as 1968, and two months before the CELAM at Medellín, nineteen lay apostolates met in the Peruvian city of Naña and issued a statement that read in part:

> It is our opinion that the real violence of the present day is the intolerable and perduring violence of an institutionalized nature. This seems clear from the facts before us: the rate of infant mortality, the lack of daily sustenance, the wage level and salary policy, the scheme of charitable contributions, and international economic relationships.[52]

This was written before the onset of terrorist violence in the 1980s, yet its message is particularly applicable today. The women of El Agustino respond to the need for the personal development of the residents of the barrio. Their goal is to keep generating ideas and organizations that will work toward the freeing of people from lives of servitude.

The Peruvian church has become much more conservative in recent years. Various factors, most especially the appointment of several conservative bishops and the Vatican's questioning of liberation theology, have contributed to this transformation. One result has been the church moving away from a passionate call for the actualization of the liberating power of the Gospel. In defiance of this trend, the women of El Agustino intensified their efforts to bring the Gospel alive in the barrio. The palliative efforts of the hierarchy are not enough and they recognize this dilemma.

Although these women are acutely aware of the repression of a machismo society and a patriarchal church, these are never the major motivating factors for their praxis. The social setting in which they live is plangent with sexual assault and violence toward women and discrimination based on sex. This gives rise to a continual questioning of self-worth and personal dignity, as well as causing an alienation of identity. Yet it is not *in spite of*, but rather *because of*, these experiences that they develop an emotional and intellectual identification with the women and with the men they serve. "I suppose that everything we do has some positive affect on our lives," said Sra. Torres. "However, the condition of being poor and being a women in Peru makes it very easy to relate to all of those around us who suffer."[53]

Said María Ramos Vega, "What we need is not a society with many more wealthy people but a place in which the very idea of poverty is acceptable and embraced. In other words, our whole approach to life should not be one of making sure that I, personally, have as much as possible but that we all meet our basic needs."[54] Esther Arteago Serrano continued on this theme:

> My mother (Benedicta) has a little plaque that says, "Poverty is no disgrace. It *is* inconvenient." She does not mean to lessen the dehumanizing influence of poverty. But she will not admit that

> it is a disgrace, because *we* are poor. I remember her telling us, when food was not available, that Jesus invites each one of us to give up what we have in this world and to help those who are poor. Look, we are poor helping those who are more poor. If everyone did this, no one would go hungry or homeless or die unnecessarily because of the lack of a common medicine.[55] (Emphasis added.)

The women here begin to unfold the utopian vision for which they work. They do not participate in SEA for economic gain. They do work for a time when each individual possesses all that is necessary to meet her basic needs. The grievous nature of poverty in El Agustino is a contradiction to the teachings of Jesus and the women intend to use everything in their power to alleviate this lamentable state. Their answer to the culture of wealth, so easily observed in their own city, is to work to change the societal order so that those who have been oppressed for centuries may be freed.

"We must not now or ever accept death by starvation or lack of basic medical care as moral," stated Brigida Weiler, a German Medical Missionary sister who has worked with the poor in Peru since 1980. "Whatever we do will be legitimized by our efforts to eliminate this possibility."[56] These are prophetic voices crying out against unfair structures and selfish individualism. In addition, these are people who refuse to admit that how they live—a purposeful decision to live poorly—is disgraceful. When poverty is no longer a life-threatening problem,[57] the women will move on to other issues. In the meantime, poverty exists in the paradoxical sphere of how they decide to live and how they choose to fight.

Subversive Memory

I get so frustrated at times that I just have to sit down and cry.

Modesta Centano Salazar

The theology to which the women of SEA give birth does not come without pain. No matter what the accomplishments of the past may be, and they have been admirable, the adverse conditions of the barrio always loom in the present and in the future. This process of creating this theology requires an unmitigated immersion into some of humanity's most atrocious circumstances. Yet this is the way in which they bring a religious vision into reality for their neighbors. They are cognizant of their goals and they use their reflective moments to understand and sustain the passion that allows them to proceed.

The process that some have called "reclaiming your voice"[58] invariably presents the need for recalling whence one comes. This history must involve the acknowledgment of the negative, dehumanizing images and concepts of women that are perpetuated in society and in the church. For example, in a country in which 62 percent of the female population is *mestiza*[59] (Amerindian and European and/or African), the feminine ideal is portrayed in advertisements as blond, tall, and thin; in other words, the direct opposite of the majority of women. Each day, in dozens of newspapers throughout the country, a scantily clad woman takes up the front page. Billboards in El Agustino never depict a *mestiza* but could be mistaken for a billboard in North America or Europe.

According to data published by the *Delegación de mujeres* (Women's Delegation), a United Nations-appointed committee, 56 percent of the reports of violent crimes filed between 1989 and 1993 were made by women against their husbands.[60] *Movimiento Manuela Ramos* (Manuela Ramos ["everywoman"] Movement) reported in 1996 an average of thirty-eight cases of sexual violence per month in Lima.

During 1997, in conjunction with Fujimori's population control campaign, *Coordinadora Nacional de Derechos Humanos* (National Coordinator of Human Rights or CNDDHH and the *Centro de la Mujer Peruana Flora Tristan* (Flora Tristan Peruvian Woman's Center) reported widespread involuntary sterilization of poor women.[61] Malnutrition is estimated at 72 percent higher for girls than for boys,[62] the majority of illiterates are women,[63] and women account for 53 percent of heads of households.[64]

These conditions have worsened in recent years. These are the histories of the women, the stories that form their memories and their present state of being. For a woman to be stunned or even paralyzed by such plights would be understandable. The women in El Agustino elect to use these facts as motivation for moving ahead. They possess survival characteristics that are nurtured by their work and reflection. In a society and church that are sexist, racist, and classist, they have survived under the worst of conditions without neglecting their commitment to family and community.

This is the foundation from which voice is developed, from which the sense of self begins to emerge from within and not from external definitions, and where subjective knowledge is nourished. There is a conscious decision to move outside of the given role and allotted space across the societal chasm that restricts them. The possibility of accomplishment is never assured yet it is just this possibility that provides motivation. "I have learned to see the world through my own eyes," said Relinda Sosa Perez.

> Before, I always followed what everyone said I should be doing. I understood, I think, how I felt but this did not seem

> to match how I was supposed to think. There is a real sense of becoming a person for the first time and I was not certain how to react to this. I also began to realize that I do things differently because I am a woman. Thanks be to God, I had all of these wonderful women here to help me along the way.[65]

The women undergo a stage of preparation in their fight for justice that openly names the "differentness" they live—as women, as *mestizas*, as the poor, as social activists, and as community leaders. This fight is fueled by anguish, anger, and fear as well as by hope, forbearance, and trust in a God-inspired mission. Their theology emerges with a focus toward particular issues and contexts as opposed to a more academic, systematic approach. They enter into a critical dialogue with all aspects of society and church that do not prove legitimate to the test in their lives. All theories—all *theological* theories—are measured against their ability to create a society in which life may be lived more fully.

Remembering the Past, Understanding the Present, and Looking toward the Future

> *You have to appreciate that we have moved from being concerned with getting food on the table for our family to feeding thousands, to training people and creating jobs, working for change in the barrio and city, looking ahead to a truly better world. I can't imagine that I ever thought this was possible.*
>
> Carmen Fernández Cano
> Economic secretary for her township

The recent past feels very distant to many of the women due to the magnitude of abrupt and society-shaking changes brought forth by internal migration and displacement, the terrorism, the hyperinflation, and the resettlement process of millions in the city of Lima. "Ten years ago, my friend lived in the *altiplano* (the high-altitude plateau) with no electricity, no running water, and they grew most of what they ate," said Celia Sánchez Rojas, secretary-general of her township. "Today she cleans government offices in a fifteen-story building with an elevator."[66]

The last half of the twentieth century brought extraordinary changes worldwide but few places have undergone such dramatic shifts as Lima. There is an understandable yearning on the part of some for times gone by. There is also a longing to re-create some of the familial and societal characteristics that were lost in the urban move. Family structures have been weakened. Mobility, virtually unknown by previous generations, is common. Desires on the part of many are rooted in material acquisitions. These are not situations unique to Peru. Nevertheless, the manner in which the women of SEA handle these changes is more unusual:

"What I have discovered," said Sra. Centano,

> is that God does not stay the same either. We were taught in grade school that God is always the same. But for me, that is putting God in a box. We cannot do that. In some ways, I have stopped trying to understand life and have starting *living* life more. Life is the gift God has given me and I had better start taking care of the gift. Life is what I hope to pass on to my children.[67] (Emphasis added.)

The gift and grace of life are intertwined with the transcendence of God. The self-offer of God, in turn, is recognized in their desire to work for the reign of God in the here and now, and to have an ever-enriching understanding of that call. In accepting the call to this end, they also accept the idea that it embraces absolutely every aspect of their existence—their work, prayer, family life, and leisure time.

The efforts to retrieve some of the aspects of life that did not survive the recent decades continue. In addition, there is the struggle of the women to maintain their own identity as individuals. Arrival and survival in Lima is precarious at best, and the daily challenges—housing, food, and clothing—were the same as they experienced in their home provinces. Yet here, everything is new and unknown. The internal immigration continues today and it is the women of SEA, who have already lived through their own turbulent period, who provide the assistance necessary for survival. Work is central to survival yet many of the new immigrants possess skills that are domestic or inapplicable to the urban environment.

The preservation of personal identity comes primarily from the relationships they build with those who live in similar circumstances. Uncertainty, insecurity, and jealousy are obvious and expected outcomes of the migratory process. The process of working through these hindrances to the point of building community requires fortitude and a true sense of reconciliation.

Sra. Bravo explains the significance of their participating in such collective efforts as a *Club de Madres* or *Vaso de Leche*:

> At first, many of the women become involved in these organizations in order to survive, literally! They arrived with two or six or ten children and often without a husband or boyfriend. The experience of loneliness is overwhelming. But

> I have seen again and again a change occur. They come to understand that the means of survival involves community. It involves all of us working together to achieve something. And through this process, slowly at times, we can see the women gaining a sense of their identity as women, and as mothers and providers and protectors. What was entirely private in the home provinces becomes both public and continues to be life giving.[68]

Equally importantly, however, is the effort made to understand the Spirit that propels them. The spirit of the women moves them out of the private, interior space into the world as it exists at this moment. The understanding of salvation is never privatized and, by making it public, they and their God are taken to the streets. "This is why I tell my children that poverty itself is not a bad thing," stated Sra. Serrano. "It is the causes of poverty that are bad. In poverty, though, we may discover so much about ourselves and our God. These are real people we live with—not just statistics. And we are all connected as creatures of God."[69]

The connection of which Sra. Serrano speaks implies an understanding that God is encountered in the historical condition. The condition of their past was one in which the spiritual journey and the transcendent movement toward God were confined more to the private sphere. This was the religious tradition brought and infused by the Spanish. The women have come to the understanding that the private aspects of faith were only a partial element of their search for the truth. In order to strive for a more fruitful journey they must work for the realization of human good. But this is partial too. There is no expectation that the ultimate good will be achieved, recognizing that this will only come through the hand of God. Nevertheless, their histories—their stories—reveal the constant presence of, and the closeness to, God that they achieve by working for the good of their neighbors. As María Ramos Vega states:

> Since I have been participating in the running and organizing of the dining rooms, I have learned a lot. We do everything we can for those who are suffering but we realize that God completes the action. I will never understand fully if this is really what God wants but through my prayer and my work, I have come to an understanding that it is. And we do all of this together—the organizers, the people who benefit from the programs, and God. Through all of this, I have felt transformed.[70]

There exist also an understanding that the involvement of the women will take them beyond the confines of the barrio into the governmental,

NGO, and ecclesiastical structures of the city and country. The intermingling of the profane and sacred is understood and accepted as necessary for the achievement of God's reign. In this way, the church of God exists in the parish, in the office, and on the streets.

Conclusion

The women's option of the poor and for the poor, the *crucis theologicus* they embrace, opens up many avenues for a deeper understanding of the mystery of God. In their use of biblical sources, they have come to understand that listening to, as well as caring for, others is inextricably linked to our religious tradition. The social activism they practice, in turn, encourages them to yearn for more. The obstacles they face—sexism, classism, and racism, among others—do not put an end to their commitment but are used as hermeneutical tools to proceed onward.

Their contemplation of God and their context results in both an embracing and thoughtful criticism of the institutional church. The faith they live engenders a deeper exploration of their lives and a realization of the need to respond to the dehumanizing conditions in which they live. In their response to their world, their thoughts and words materialize into action that can be felt, indeed heard, throughout the barrio.

A careful listening to their words leads us to prioritize the primary factors in their rhetoric and actions and it encourages us to understand what is said and what may remain unsaid. In our examination of *la llamada de Dios*, the role of tradition, the presence of conversion and hope, and the primacy of dialogue, we see a concrete definition of the poor. This interpretation permits us to see the existence of nonpersonhood in their environment—a sense of nonbeing that each one of the women has personally experienced. Their desire to preserve and promote life counteracts the anonymity forced upon the poor. It also promotes the dignity of each human being and lifts up the circumstance of being poor, while simultaneously condemning and struggling against the causes of poverty.

In their recollections, the women have faced head-on the formidable odds they encounter as women, as the poor, and as agents of change. In this fashion too, we witness the rekindling of a sense of identity—for themselves and for those for whom they struggle. Intertwined with their work is an ever-growing sense of the spirit of God, which sustains them and presses them onward. God is encountered in the historical situation and it is this encounter that we will now examine in detail.

CHAPTER 4

The Theology

We have examined the way in which the women of *Servicios Educativos El Agustino* (Educational Services El Agustino or SEA) exist in a constantly changing, challenging, and pluralistic environment. Crucial to our understanding of their theology is that it, too, is evolving in the same diverse climate. Since this theology does not emerge from the traditional realm of academia, there is a necessary emphasis on doing, as opposed to writing, a theology. As German theologian Ursula King, states, "To use a traditional distinction, the process of theologizing occurs inductively rather than deductively."[1]

Inasmuch as these women, for the most part, do not have access to formal theological education, the essence of their work is determined through their actions and through their reflections on what they do and why. In the same manner, their theological analysis does not necessarily fit into the categories of the academy. This furnishes an opportunity to understand a theology from the underside of history.

Their theology emanates from their critique of, and struggle against, the oppression in which they and their neighbors exist. Their use of traditional sources—the Bible, church documents, tradition, culture, reflection, and the like—affords the opportunity to explore the interpretation of those whose voices have not been heard.

To grasp the theology of the women of El Agustino, we must recognize that theologies come forth in many forms. Their theology is clearly anthropological in that it is distinctly a product of their particular culture, time, and place. All theologies are culturally, historically, and socially conditioned, yet the uniquely challenging environment of this barrio produces circumstances that give rise to singular human activity that is analyzed a posteriori.

Where, then, is the influence of God felt if theology is the work of human beings? Theologian Kathryn Tanner suggests, "Such a question is . . . no harder (or easier) to answer when expressed in cultural terms than it is when expressed, as it has been for the last several centuries, in terms of modern Western historical consciousness."[2]

In coming to a greater understanding of themselves and their world, the women of this study are compelled to weave a vision of life that permits the possibility of moving beyond the desperate poverty, rampant violence, and institutional repression in which they exist. This process of understanding leads them onto a path seeking awareness that possesses manifest theological propositions.

Tanner again broaches an important question: "Does (a theology) help people successfully navigate their world and cope effectively with life's vicissitudes?"[3] In a place where "no one . . . stays young for long" and "at every corner of its chaotic and dangerous streets, alcohol and drugs are for sale,"[4] *vicissitudes* hardly begin to depict the formidable quandaries and barriers the people of El Agustino face.

In spite of the monumental obstacles—or conceivably because of them and the perseverance with which the women assail them—there comes a greater understanding of the enigmatic lives that they lead. This provides fertile ground for the augmentation of the attendant conditions in which theology is done.

While in the past it was a question of what school of philosophy was used as a hermeneutical tool, herein we discover life circumstances as the lens through which interpretation comes to pass. This, of course, is no different from the theologizing of the early Christians. They too struggled with their specific cultural environment in order to come to an understanding of their faith. For both the early Christians and the women of El Agustino, together with innumerable groups in between, the significance and applicability of a particular theology is dependent upon its relationship with a particular time and place.

A theology also must reflect certain signs of the universal. The particulars provide an entrance point to the universal. "There is no reason to think that theology's being set in a Christian cultural context rules out theological claims that are universal in scope. Because theology operates within a Christian context is no reason to think theologians are discussing matters that only concern Christians."[5] The contexts of violence, subjugation, disenfranchisement, poverty, and sexism may be the source of theological reflection in multiple countries, cultures, and religions.

Tanner writes of a "theology in everyday life" that both challenges the output of trained theologians and sanctions theology to be directly applicable to the life issues and concerns of those other than the educated elite. The theology of which she speaks lends itself to the understanding of personal actions, the values that are upheld, and the signs of the times that provide meaningful impetus. In this fashion, the action that is undertaken—the praxis—becomes the source from which theological interpretation occurs. As an example, she suggests that theology may be found "embedded in such matters as the way altar and pews are arranged."[6]

In El Agustino, it is found in the manner in which lives are saved, despair is lessened, lives are given new meaning, and the possibility of living life fully is encouraged.

In the women's quest to understand the value of their suffering, their relationships with the institutional church, their affirmation of life, and their interpretation and integration of the word of God, they clearly make assertions regarding their God and God's presence in their lives. Additionally, they plainly delineate the import of the belief they have and the values they uphold.

It does not take a great deal of intellectual thought for them to recognize the ungodliness of multiple determinants in their lives in the barrio. It does, however, require astute discernment to come to a point at which they are capable of waging battle against the sinful structures they face.

Their starting point remains those factors that stand in conflict with the exegesis of their Christian faith. There are no abstract beginnings but rather the often cruel reality of their lives. If their theology appears somewhat less clear or less systematic than that of the academy, it is for the simple reason that survival at times makes clarity and systematicity nigh impossible.

The poor, who have become agents of their own destiny in El Agustino, are presenting challenges to the classical role of theology in the academy. Their theologizing becomes more complex with the passage of time, as the liberation they seek emerges as a clearer reality. In consideration of the evolving nature of their theology, their work may be considered at the beginning stages of an emerging theology. However, the breadth of their labors already confronts more than the socioeconomic and political oppression that are familiar territory to those working to free humanity from oppressive structures. The women of El Agustino, in particular, understand the necessity of a concentration on ethnic, cultural, sexual, and racial oppression, as well.

Their activities represent a reinterpretation of the meaning of salvation and their reflections expose the desires that motivate their work. The prevalence of sin within their midst also provides the impetus to recognize God's abundant grace and salvific promise. On the one hand, they fully accept themselves as God's creatures and as recipients of God's free grace. However, they also conclusively acknowledge the call of God, the answer to which is an indispensable element on the road to salvation. To imitate Christ is sacrosanct.

Through their labor, we have examined the consciousness-raising activity that is a prominent source of their theological thought. This involves the affirmation and promotion of life, an elucidation of the word of God in novel and challenging ways, the use of their own suffering to promote their understanding of God's presence, and the confrontation of those elements intrinsic to their society that stand in opposition to Gospel values. These are the sources we must further examine in order to come to a more complete understanding of the theology of the women of El Agustino. As Fr. Gustavo Gutiérrez stated, they are the best of liberation theologians because they live the Gospel.

Origins

The way in which the women of El Agustino do theology encompasses an action different from that of the academy. It entails a submersion into the context of one's society as well as a thorough understanding of one's self and community. This is the starting point for all theology and the truth expounded by a theology relates to the level of its involvement in the contextual circumstances.

The complex nature of theology is made even more so by the consideration of cultural, religious, economic, and political influences. However, these deliberations in turn make the theological enterprise more sound. As theologians, these women are affected by their existence under oppressive structures. By nature, the oppression they experience calls for a reconsideration of the philosophical standard of a theology, be it transcendental, existential, analytic, phenomenological, or Thomist.

The theological venture demands a sincere and dedicated intellectual effort, as exemplified by the communal and individual reflections of the women. These reflections are necessarily focused on the tribulations of the women and their neighbors that are a major component of their lives. It is to this reality of suffering we now turn.

What Suffering Teaches Us

At the dawn of the third millennium, it is impossible to theologize genuinely without incorporating the suffering endured by the human race. When the world has at its disposal every resource necessary to eliminate abject poverty, hunger, and homelessness—as well as the despair that accompanies these—we are challenged to answer why we have not done so. When the dignity of millions—a dignity reaffirmed by numerous government constitutions, thousands of organizations, as well as the church—is shattered by conditions we can change, those who ponder their faith are required to ask why this has not been accomplished.

The people of the Northern Hemisphere labor industriously to eliminate all forms of suffering, with untold billions of dollars spent to find cures for non-life-threatening ailments. Suffering is viewed as such an "evil" that certain activists toil to legalize doctor-assisted suicide.[7] This occurs while people, such as the women of SEA, labor to obtain the cup of milk that will save a child's life. In societies where sexism and classism actively work against the possibility of living life fully, marketing schemes throughout the world implicitly and explicitly promote these societal norms. The incongruity of this contemporary phenomenon must not be ignored. This is the challenge that all theologians face today.

Without some emphasis on the wretchedness of the human condition in one's community and throughout the world, a theology lacks the authenticity to call itself that. The women accomplish a very accurate reading of the Gospel of Jesus Christ, and they live out the familiar passage, "Whatever you did for one of the least of these brothers of mine, you did for me" (Matt 25:40). Each specific context, as well as the world in general, demands the attention of all disciplines in respect to the dehumanizing conditions in which the majority of the world lives. Søren Kierkegaard understood this necessity, and the barriers one faces, when he wrote:

> The moment I take Christianity as a doctrine and so indulge my cleverness or profundity or my eloquence or my imaginative powers in depicting it, people are very pleased; I am looked upon as a serious Christian. The moment I begin to express existentially what I say, and consequently to bring Christianity into reality, it is just as though I have exploded existence—the scandal is there at once.[8]

Expressing existentiality, to use Kierkegaard's words, is no longer an option but an incontestable demand by Christianity itself. In other words, the process of thinking theologically must involve the intellectual and the concrete together with the action that is demanded by the Gospel. This is how a "theology in everyday life" emerges.

I will use theologian M. Shawn Copeland's well-grounded definition of suffering as a foundation for this section. She writes: "Suffering is the disturbance of our inner tranquility caused by physical, mental, emotional, and spiritual forces that we grasp as jeopardizing our lives, our very existence. Evil is the negation and deprivation of good; suffering, while never identical with evil, is inseparable from it."[9]

The "seductiveness" of suffering may be substantiated by a cursory view of newspapers, magazines, and television reports in any locale. While these accounts rarely go to the root of any particular cause, unless it is a natural phenomenon such as a hurricane or fire, suffering itself is deemed newsworthy and appeals to the general population. With current abilities to report news instantaneously from the most remote location in the world, we are fed a daily diet of the appalling conditions in which so much of the world exists. The fact that people are suffering is an undeniable fact. Also irrefutable is the reality that much of the world has become immune to the daily reports of these ravages.

The women of SEA go beyond a state of mere awareness of suffering in their community. They suffer, they struggle to relieve the suffering of others, and they work toward a more complete understanding of suffering's origins and remedies. In many cases, the root causes of the debilitating conditions may be found in societal structures that have been handed down over the centuries. These systemic forms of oppression are often embedded deeply in the cultural and societal compositions of a particular time and place. Dismantling them is a formidable task. However, this does not prevent the women from working to eradicate these structures. They often stand alone in this task.

The wealthier citizens of their country (and elsewhere) often fail or refuse to acknowledge the degree of suffering that exists here. Those who possess the ability to make a difference often spiritualize their lives as Christians to avoid dealing with the "existentiality" that blatantly confronts them. They may ascribe their stance to Jesus' words, "You will always have the poor among you" (John 12:8).[10] Perhaps they sense that the problems of the poor are beyond their capacity to respond. Or conceivably, it is the incomprehensibility of the pain that the poor endure that prevents corrective, charitable action on their part.[11]

The effort to understand suffering, however, provides a unique opportunity. As Copeland also writes, "Quite paradoxically, the suffering caused by evil can result in interior development and perfection as well as in social and cultural good."[12] The wealthy and the powerful forfeit the opportunity to experience growth when they do not follow a similar path toward an understanding of the relationship between suffering and Christianity. Their lack of consideration of this relationship, in turn, creates an even greater distance between the lives of the poor and the nonpoor.

No matter how inexpressible suffering may be, the women understand that the task of relieving it should be taken on as an integral element of their Christian lives. "To understand El Agustino," said Ofelia Montes López, the director of SEA,

> you must recognize that the pain the people suffer is everywhere. This does not make it a constantly unhappy place to

> live, but the pain is something we must identify and address. When you see someone who has become homeless or is not able to feed her children, there is also a sense for that person that she does not belong to the community. Here is a sense of disconnection from those around her that amplifies the negative conditions. Obviously, this affects the sense of community for everyone. Therefore, we must also address this lack of connection.[13]

In addressing the issue of people living fully, these women face the challenges of the present social condition, the historical factors they inherited, the psychological state of the barrio's residents, the disturbing economic conditions, as well as the spiritual dimensions of each person. Zenaida Zúñiga Medina, a board member of the Central Federation of *Comedores Populares* of Lima and Callao, expanded upon this when she related a story:

> A neighbor of mine was sexually assaulted when she was returning in the early morning from her job. Now she is experiencing so many emotions and questions: Was it her fault? What will her husband think if he finds out? Will it happen again? She even wonders if she will lose her job (as a housecleaner for a wealthy family) if her employers find out. This type of violence has so many grave affects. She is concerned about her family's stability, financial and otherwise, she experiences guilt for what happened, and she has asked me why God allowed this to happen to her.[14]

The last question is one with which the women of SEA must wrestle continually. How does one explain the presence of God amid such suffering? Obviously, it requires more than a simplistic "offering up" that has been the mainstay for many Christians. The women often turn to their reflections on the life of Jesus for help, as exemplified by the words of Rosa Canto Castro, a community organizer:

> If there is one message that I have received from my study of Jesus, it is that life is not always easy. I guess that this is the human life we all live. But we also learn that, after we accept pain as part of our life, we must begin to come to some understanding of pain and suffering. If you look at the causes of suffering in our neighborhood, it is easy to see that this is not the work of God. We have had many corrupt governments that caused many of the money problems we have. Machismo attitudes did not come from Jesus. Just the opposite. Loneliness,

> which is so common here, comes from all of the other conditions. But to understand this is not enough. If we are to believe we answer the call of God, we must work, work very hard, to eliminate these problems. God did not make them. Humans did. So we humans must undo them in the name of God.[15]

The words of Sra. Canto Castro depict the way in which the women's understanding of God embraces Jesus as God who has experienced human pain, and of God who calls them to transform the structures that create pain. This necessitates a moving beyond the current circumstances into a future of hope. Integral to this process is a realization that their personal suffering places them in a privileged position. As Filipino United Church of Christ pastor Eleazar S. Fernandez writes:

> Suffering, extreme suffering, is a mother of both virtue and vice: It is a mother of hope and fatalism, of faith and unfaith, of struggle and passivity. Fatalism, unfaith, and passivity are characteristic marks of a people who has not come to the awareness of the nonnecessity of their suffering, a people who have not broken the clutches of suffering without hope to embrace the kind of suffering that is pregnant with hope.[16]

It is the hope, faith, and struggle of these women that moves them out of a position of powerlessness and muteness. Creating forces to combat the causes of suffering entails using power that they do not necessarily desire. Yet they acknowledge that without the utilization of power to resist and break down dehumanizing factors, they may stand accused of complicity. Convinced of the importance of suffering—as a condition they experience, as a motivating factor in their work, as an object of analysis that focuses their work, and as an integral component of the Christian message—the significance of "fatalism, unfaith, and passivity" fades. The manner in which this happens is more difficult to explain. While theologians have developed theodicies[17] to explain a just God in a world in which so many suffer, the women of El Agustino approach the concept of evil and suffering not as a detriment to belief but rather as an impetus to deepen their faith. As Modesta Centano Salazar, secretary general of the town council, said:

> I am a single mother with a fifth-grade education and one son. When my son was a teenager, gangs started to appear and the children were gravitating toward them. We could not just sit by and watch the situation worsen. Therefore, another friend with (community organizing) experience and I joined the *Directiva Central del Pueblo* (Town Council).

> Our first responsibility was to put on a play, *El Artista* (The Artist), in which we tried to show how God created the world. In other words, God is the artist, but each one of us is like the custodian of the work of art. We each have our own interpretations. We can improve the work of art—such as giving it light so it can be seen and putting it in an environment in which it is not harmed—or we can do damage to it, like scratching it or hiding it away.
>
> We wanted the kids to know that each one of them has responsibility for the gifts that God has given them: life, family, home, faith. Even if "the painting" has been damaged, it is still possible to restore it and this is the task that each one of us has.
>
> In the process of putting on the play, I came to realize more deeply the call of God and my need to respond to it. This meant more involvement, which took me away from my son at times, interfered with my work, and cut off my free time. Therefore, I guess you could say that I "suffered" for the good. However, this is the type of suffering that is good and it breaks down whatever causes more suffering.[18]

Although sources of suffering will never be completely overcome, the resistance to making them instrumental in one's life diminishes their power. "When many of the people first arrive in El Agustino," related Soraya Ronquillo Peña, Ph.D., coordinator of the Women's Team, "there is a true sense of being absolutely powerless over the negative factors in their lives. They see the world as a tragic place in which they must simply endure human existence. However, it is almost miraculous to watch the changes that take place as they slowly chip away at this mentality."[19]

There exists a tension between the recognition of the contemporary exigency and one's projection into the future. This balance between the present in which one lives and the future for which one hopes is a common theme in the discussion of the women. Martha Vera Belleza said:

> The prophet Jeremiah was a living example of what we should be: bearers of hope and workers for hope. Through him, the Lord said, "I have plans for you. You will prosper and no harm will come to you. I have plans to give you hope for the future." (Jer. 29:11) Jeremiah was also living in very difficult times but he did not take his eyes off that future full of hope. And he worked very hard for it, too. This is what we are doing. Keeping our eye on a future that promises something better. We may not realize it all in our lifetime but we must, we absolutely must work for it now.[20]

A few of the women have read Fr. Gutiérrez's extensive work on the Book of Job[21] and all of them have used this Scripture in their biblical study or theological reflection groups. Here again, we discover examples of the analysis they provide to their social setting, in this case, the relationship between God and suffering. "What we see in Job, " remarked Celia Sánchez Rojas, secretary general of her township,

> is a man struggling to understand all that has happened to him. His example is one for all of us. In the beginning, Job is demanding answers from God and God is not responding in the way he would like. I think we have all undergone the same feeling here in El Agustino. However, Job keeps insisting that he is innocent, just as the hungry child here is innocent. In the end, we really do not have the answers we would like to receive, in Job or in El Agustino.
>
> However, Job teaches us that it is all right to question what is going on. There have been times when I am so angry with God I scream. I look to Job at those times and I know that God can handle this. (She laughs.) However, it is at times like this, if I am open to God, I feel the presence more alive than before. I cannot control *el fenómeno El Niño* and I cannot change all of the bad here. But this does not mean that God is absent. This is when God is right there beside us.[22]

The suffering the women experience personally and through their work allows them to broaden and develop their personal relationship with God. This is not, however, always the case. The women spoke of those companions who had ended their involvement with SEA for reasons of despair, lack of hope, or pressure from their families.[23] The negative conditions are not always eliminated or reduced enough for everyone. Because of this, the women must also incorporate into their reflections and work an understanding of the limitations of their abilities and influence.

They do not consider poverty itself a disgrace. Nor do they envision suffering as an irredeemable evil. The sources of poverty and of suffering are what are evil. They consider both as opening doors to the potential for grace. This gift from God in some ways allows them to transcend the presence of that which holds them and others back from lives of dignity. It permits the reality of promoting life amid distressing and antagonistic odds. It works to prevent social death *and* physical death. In the end, they choose life.

Ecclesiastical Relationships

The church sees in Mary the highest expression of the "feminine genius," and she finds in her a source of constant inspiration. Mary called herself "the handmaid of the Lord" (Luke 1:38). Through obedience to the word of God she accepted her lofty yet not easy vocation as wife and mother in the family of Nazareth.

John Paul II
Letter to attendees at the
Fourth World Conference on Women, 1995

I am convinced that women are the most discriminated in the church and it is one of the things that we want to change because the majority of the people who run the parish are women. Maybe we do not have to "change" anything—it is happening!

José Ignacio Mantecón, S.J.
former pastor, *La Virgen de Nazaret*
(The Virgin of Nazareth Parish)

The women of SEA are actively involved in the operation of the parish. They also approach their involvement with pragmatism, realistic expectations, and a critical eye. As Gloria Bravo Palomeque, a sales coordinator for a *panadería* (bakery), explains,

> It is necessary to understand that we love the priests in the parish, but we do not put them up on a pedestal. Likewise, they do not want themselves put up on a pedestal. Suggestions for new projects—Christian communities, Bible study groups, new *comedores populares* (communal dining rooms), and the like—often come from the women but the priests support us 100 percent. We struggle hand-in-hand with the priests. And they provide much leadership and support.[24]

The priests and nuns here also promoted the advancement of self-esteem and the development of skills. Irene Cáceres Sánchez was married in the church when she was 14 and had eight children by the age of 33 (1973), when her husband deserted the family. She participated in the *Comité Único Vecinal Feminino* (Women's Neighborhood Committee) in 1975 and was a founding member of the *Comité de Lucha* (Committee of Struggle) the following year. Sra. Cáceres is particularly grateful to the clergy of the parish:

> My children were very sick with tuberculosis when the Jesuits arrived in 1968. At the time, I felt that I needed to offer all of my suffering up to God and just accept it. But the Jesuits started to go out into the parish to seek out families in need. It did not matter if we went to Mass or not. For us, this was new to see a priest inquire about our personal lives, to see what was going on.
>
> The place where I lived was terrible because it had no services, and there was excrement and garbage everywhere. The priests said that we did not have to live like this. Thirty years later it sounds strange saying this, but we had never thought that way before. We began to organize and my house became a center for literacy training. The priests would help prepare us for meetings or sometimes they would just put a microphone in our hands and say, "talk." They would tell us our opinion was important no matter how it came out. We just kept on speaking until we came to believe what they told us.[25]

The women speak openly of the support they received from clergy and nuns in the barrio. Importantly, the nuns and priests encouraged the connection between what the women were doing to improve their lives and the presence of God in this work. The parish also stepped in initially as a liaison between government agencies working on improvements and the people of the barrio. "We have always been supported spiritually by the parish in the most difficult times," said Elvira Torres Anas. "When we were disappointed, we were uplifted. It has always been a continuous relationship and no one forgets the beautiful and kind things that we learned. We feel a constant presence of the church and God."[26]

"The priests and nuns in the parish have played a very important role in the development of one of the most crucial programs, the communal dining rooms," said Sra. Zúñiga. "When they were first established, SEA did not exist and the nuns and priests supplied the food to operate. We read the Bible together with (the Mother Superior of the nuns in El Agustino) and when the nuns left, we continued on."[27] Martha Vera Belleza spoke of the variety of assistance received from the parish. "Support has come in the areas of religious belief, spirituality, self-esteem, personal and organizational development, skills training, problems within the family . . . and from a sense of solidarity and hope."[28]

The situation in El Agustino also has its shadow side, exacerbated by the lack of religious men and women working in the parish, the desire on the part of the women to be more involved, and their desire to have the priests and nuns assist them in reaching beyond the theological reflection they have accomplished thus far. "It used to be that every Mother's Day," said Sra. Zúñiga, "we would have a Mass in the *comedor*. We would gather as a group and allow God to speak to us and to tell us what our mission is. But, today we do not have this. Perhaps it is because there is no priest available. Or perhaps it is because we have grown beyond this."[29]

Upon further inquiry, Sra. Zúñiga expanded upon the theme of a woman's role in the Roman Catholic Church. Although this appeared somewhat difficult for many of the women to discuss, a sense of disenfranchisement exists on their part. With their self-esteem raised and their work producing tangible results, they came to question their lack of involvement as presiders in the sacraments. This, and the lack of an ecclesiastical environment encouraging ongoing development in their theological and spiritual lives, has moved many of them away from regular attendance at Mass. Benedict "Beni" Serrano Agüero, one of the most respected social activists in Peru, said,

> When I started to work in the community, I participated in all of the Masses. I would go to several parishes. If I did not, I would not be satisfied. (But now) . . . I find the liturgies to be too simple and I have started to distance myself from the traditional forms. Little by little, I have started not to go to Mass. Instead, I have been reading the Bible, reflecting on its message, and then acting concretely. If I do not act, it is as if I am not alive.[30]

Because Sra. Serrano Agüero is held up as a model Christian by the priests in the parish, her declining attendance at liturgy is noted and influences many of the other women. Sra. Serrano Agüero said,

> I have transmitted my faith to my family and friends with my attitude. I always motivate them to give thanks to God for allowing us to eat and to work and giving us the strength to continue on. I have told my children since they were little that God loves them. Jesus died on the cross for us and now lives in our hearts. I speak to them about the message of the Bible—and I believe that there is no greater message than to give one's life for others. This is my calling.[31]

The great needs of the barrio are never far from view and many of the women feel that the parish needs to become more involved in the solutions. "I think the church needs to reaffirm itself more with the community," stated Relinda Sosa Perez, a coordinator of a neighborhood *comedor*. "There are other denominations going door-to-door trying to get you to change denominations. We must be sure to have an understanding so that our beliefs, our work, and our challenges may be brought together in the Catholic faith."[32]

With the rise in self-esteem, the sense of possessing a valuable opinion, and the need to move constantly onward in their theological quest, the women have begun to question their own practice of religion. Through their praxis within the barrio, they discover an endless source of explication of the mystery of God. They have grown accustomed to, and desirous of, the process of self-challenge and come to find their parish liturgies a weak link in this regard. The locus of their insight into God has been firmly established in their biblical studies, praxis, communal reflections, and individual prayer.

Only here we can truly begin to understand their movements. When their work involves life or death questions, the immediacy of the religious experience—if so desired—is omnipresent. They do not consider religion to be the enemy of progress nor antithetical to their goals. Yet, the parish in El Agustino—*their* church—has succeeded in establishing an environment in which "thinking the faith" comes naturally. Gutiérrez's question of how to speak of God to those who have been trod upon, abandoned, and left without hope is answered by the women.[33] In the answering process, the women's hunger for further theological development is heightened. This inexorably involves a systematic analysis of their faith, a progressively deeper comprehension of God's presence in what they do, and a sustaining of hope against great odds. In other words, the routine liturgy or standard homily does not always meet their needs. Doctrinal faith misses the mark. These women ask for the level of stimulation that will advance their doing of God's work while simultaneously nourishing their doing of theology.

The women have discovered that the lives of each other provide notable measures of inspiration and hope. When they do encounter uncertainty, a state all too common in this oppressive neighborhood, they understand the needfulness of waiting, praying, and searching for the light that will lead them out of the darkness. This is an example of the wisdom of human love and of a very intimate relationship with God. God is not *other* than the human experience but is experienced most profoundly in the depths of the human experience. "Our creed tells us that Jesus descended into hell before he rose on the third day. This is not merely a poetic allusion," asserts Ofelia Montes, "but the manner in which we may come to an understanding of the hell we sometimes personally encounter. If Jesus did this for us, can we not do the same for Jesus?"[34]

Herein we discover the challenge that the women present to the church and the one they create for themselves. If the church in El Agustino is to continue to fulfill its function as an instrument to guide and support the faith of the people, it must respond ever more intelligently to the needs of the people. (Indeed, this may well be applied to parishes throughout the world.) And if the women are to continue the ever-expanding exploration and understanding of their faith, they may move ahead in ways that continue to remove them from the sacramental life of the church until the church itself responds adequately. Once again, we witness a gift—and a challenge—that emanates from the women.

Affirmation of Life

> *I guess you could say that the starting point for everything we do is life: its protection, promotion, preservation, enhancement.*
>
> Rosa Pacheco
> Coordinator
> Federación Popular de Mujeres
> (Federation of Women)

"There is one business in El Agustino that always does well," said Sra. Serrano Agüero, "*la funeraria* (the funeral home)." Death is no stranger to the residents of this barrio. Neither is disease that could be prevented with common medicines, homelessness that would require minimal funds to correct, hunger that demands just a slight change in the balance of resources to abolish, as well as child neglect, the lack of educational possibilities, basic electrical and sewer services, and opportunities to support oneself and one's family. The protection, promotion, preservation, and enhancement of life, using Sra. Pacheco's words, is a primary theological activity for the women.

The primacy of this emphasis on life is lessened by those who are either ignorant of, or unable to respond theologically to, the inhuman conditions in which so much of the world exists. As theologian José Comblin wrote, when theology emanates principally from the First World, "it ha(s) to claim to present a total view of human beings and their place in the world."[35]

It is obvious that many theologies, for whatever reasons, fail to consider the state of a majority of the world's population. The emphasis on life of the theology of the women of El Agustino fulfills a need implied in all theologies.

Some people are untouched by the presence of suffering in the world, and the culture of death in numerous countries is perceived as nothing more than the status quo. It is not uncommon to hear more well-to-do citizens of Lima lament that the poor step out of their *barriadas*.[36] The common perception is that the causes of poverty are not the problem but the poor themselves. Herein exists a sad distortion of humans created in *imago Dei*. "The image in which the poor are created," one might hear in a prosperous barrio, "is different from the image in which I am created."

The *llamada de Dios* (call of God) to which the women respond manifests itself initially in the confession of the sacredness of every life. Inherent in this process is the hope for the future and the recognition of being able to give rise to policies, structures, interventions, and simple acts that help to diminish the culture of death. "We learned in catechism when we were young," said Modesta Centano Salazar, "that Jesus, by dying on the cross and rising again on the third day, overcame death forever. We also learned that we were to imitate Jesus in every way possible. Well, if I can work to save just one life from hunger or solitude, I feel that I am imitating Christ."[37]

Fundamental to an understanding of the work of the women is the recognition of God's sacred gift of life. "I often encounter people who feel that life is no longer worth living," recounted Lucy Mejia Calderón, a coordinator of *comedores*. "I am sometimes tempted to ask them, 'But what about the alternative?'

> But this is where we find our mission—to change things so that the wonderful gift we have received from God is considered something precious by everyone. And if you have something precious, you take very good care of it.
>
> We encounter sin every day of our lives. I could move away and join a *claustro* (cloister) to get away from it. I think, however, that we are called to be a part of creation. We must not run away from the world and all its problems but become active in the world. This is how we will make it to heaven.[38]

Sra. Mejia Calderón challenges the body/spirit dualism that has been a focus of some theologies of the Northern Hemisphere. Through her emphasis on the incarnational, she also mirrors Ignatius Loyola's behest to find God in all things. Holiness is not something to be found solely in church or in private prayer, but also, even more so, in the work with God's disenfranchised. "What is the purpose of life?" asked Sra. Torres Anas. "Well, I think God wants us to enjoy the gift we have been given. But we cannot enjoy it; we should not enjoy it fully, if those around us are in pain, for whatever reason. And I truly believe that by helping others, I get to enjoy my life more."[39]

Sra. Torres Anas's words reflect her consideration of the purpose of life and our individual and communal responsibility to respond to its antithesis. This is an indication of God's grace and how it enters human life. The form in which this grace may appear is as ineffable and mysterious as God is; yet it is also as incarnate as the world in which we live. Essential to accepting and embracing the grace of God, however, is a demeanor of openness. "We talk about San Ignacio and his wish to find God in all things," related Sra. Montes López, "but this is much more difficult than it sounds." She continues:

> There are times that I am in situations that turn my stomach. Disease ravages the body and the smells of a dying person are dreadful. At times like that, I think of San Pedro Claver. I am told that he licked the wounds of the African slaves to whom he ministered when he was repulsed by their condition. This helps to give me strength at the times I want to run away. Can you understand this? I believe that when we push ourselves beyond what we thought we were capable of, that is when we experience God the most. That is when we lose the "self" in every good sense of the word. I have read enough psychology to know that this is not accepted in certain circles. However, to be Christian calls for this losing of the "self" in love and concern for the other. This is the occasion for discovering more of yourself than you thought possible.[40]

The question of one being open to God's love and self-disclosure is ultimately quite personal. The lives of the women consistently expose them to the possibility of change—transformations unexpected, challenging, and life giving. In this way, there is the potential for a deeper understanding of what it means to be human, to be a creature of God. There exists, too, the possibility of discerning what it means for a human to direct her life toward Jesus. Relinda Sosa Perez described the act of focusing one's life in this manner:

> I think we all understand that there is a great deal about life that we do not understand. Why am I working here instead of trying to get a job that pays more money? Why was I dedicating more and more of my time to the *comedor* but not knowing really if it was for good or bad? Why am I Catholic but I do not go to Mass? Why do I go to the church to cry and pray when I feel depressed? Why has my relationship with my children and my husband improved since I started working with the projects of SEA? Why do I feel closer to God than I ever have before?
>
> I think the answer lies in the fact that, after years of fighting what I thought I should be doing, I have left myself available to Jesus. I am not perfect. I make many mistakes. But I keep on trying to hear the voice of God directing my work.[41]

The women place an emphasis in the fight against the exploitation of the people of El Agustino. For example, one of the few skills that the people can offer is their hard labor. They often experience in the workplace a subjugation that exploits their neediness. The indigenous population has been placed in a position of servitude since the time of the Spanish colonizers. The women, most of whom are dark complexioned, spoke of being taken to restaurants by a non-Amerindian friend and not being served. The public transportation systems are set up so that a minimum of buses operates directly between poor and wealthy neighborhoods. The poor women who work in wealthy homes are required to take circuitous routes to their places of employment, often consuming three or four hours of their time daily.

The economy of Peru leaves few options for addressing the problems faced by the poor. Yet, without the skills and education necessary to advance, the poor remain poor. There is little federal funding to create new educational programs. The ones that currently exist are strained by budgetary limitations and these programs are low in the priority of the government.

Jaime O'Leary, S.J. was a national administrator for *Fe y Alegría—Movimiento de Educación Popular Integral* (Faith and Joy—Popular Educational Movement). He is currently principal of a *Fe y Alegría* school in Jaen, Peru, one of a nationwide program of elementary, secondary, and vocational training schools in impoverished areas. The church has responded to some of the many needs of the poor and disenfranchised. As he remarked:

> *Fe y Alegría* currently has 45 schools and 55,000 students throughout Peru. All of our schools are in areas where no other school exists or in urban areas where the existing schools would not be able to meet the needs of the impoverished population or they do not accept the poor.
>
> Our goals reflect the greatest needs of the poor: promoting the awareness of their potential, allowing them to realize that they can be agents of their own change, and involving them in the creation of a new society whose structures make possible a commitment of Christian faith in works of love and justice. Although we receive some funding from international NGOs and from the Catholic Church, the yearly expenditure per student is less than US$70.[42]

Fr. O'Leary's comments reemphasize that the social demeanor of the poor is one of alienation, and the funds to institute changes for the better are lacking. SEA, accordingly, works for the promotion of the dignity of workers. While you will hear such claims of new programs from political parties during campaigns, the reality exposes the lie behind those words. "It is to the advantage of the rich to keep the poor impoverished," said Sra. Cáceres. "The only value that we poor feel we possess is our ability to work. By keeping us poor, we maintain a sense of impotence and we are desperate to take any kind of work, no matter how demeaning."[43]

Due to the ever-present influence of machismo attitudes, women are particularly vulnerable to the phenomenon of subjugation. The androcentric emphasis of Peruvian society, exhibited in multiple ways, is certainly not challenged by the patriarchy of the church. While the situation in *La Virgen de Nazaret* parish is uniquely better than most, many still cannot look to the church for examples of women as *imago Dei*. Fortunately, the women of SEA present images of women who are breaking the rules, making changes, and growing in the process. "Can you understand the fact that just 10 years ago," asked fifty-five-year-old Martha Vera Belleza, "I did not even think of speaking in front of my husband's friends. I was there to make them food. Today, I have a microphone in my hand in front of hundreds of men and women."[44]

Brazilian activist Fr. Paulo Freire wrote of the human toll inflicted by the colonization of peoples throughout the world: "Every act of conquest implied a conqueror and someone or something which is conquered. The conqueror imposes his objectives on the vanquished, and makes of them his possession. He imposes his own contours on the vanquished, who internalize this shape and become ambiguous beings 'housing' another."[45] Freire emphasizes the often-indecipherable forces that are at work with those who have been historically oppressed. The societal structures that promote oppression are more easily identified than the psychological, internalized forces that the oppressed carry with them. In other words, the heritage of oppression may result in the oppressed cooperating unconsciously in their own oppression. Freire argues that even the most obvious paths toward liberation may be ignored or not given credence because of the culture of domination.[46]

Slowly, projects in El Agustino and elsewhere are struggling to remove the yoke of this "vanquishment." The women make concerted efforts to assure that how they name themselves, how they define their own being, is not merely the imposition of definitions and names from the outside. It is here that we discover the "hermeneutical spiral." As their efforts to solve the problems of the barrio bear fruit, they themselves benefit and grow. In this furthering of development and understanding—that is, the spiral ascending—they are able to bring forward fresh ideas and concepts. Pivotal to this growth and development is the remembering whence they came—a place of disenfranchisement, weakness, and unworthiness. "It seems almost too obvious to say," related Sra. Montes López, "but when we keep our eye on where we have come from, we are more certain not to do anything to others that has been done to us."[47]

The women are working to create a new humanity out of the detritus they inherited from the colonizers and from multiple corrupt governments. They do not expect to experience complete success in their lifetime but as Rosa Castillo Reyes, president of the *Club de Madres* (Mothers' Club), said:

> We look ahead to a time when our children and our children's children will never have to experience the *escollos* (pitfalls or obstacles) that we have. I was quite old before I started developing a sense of self-worth. However, my daughter is just a teenager and she already knows that she is a very special creature of God. She can accomplish great things if she works hard enough.[48]

The Role of Scripture

The starting point for the women of SEA in reading and interpreting the Bible is stated by Paulina Flores de Osorio:

> We women have come to understand from our experiences in parishes throughout the country—remember that people from all over Peru live in El Agustino—that the word of God is not always used to promote the freedom of God's people. However, we no longer just sit and accept what is handed over to us. Now, we go to the Bible ourselves. In order to be faithful to the word of God and faithful to the community, we must reflect on the Bible in the light of the community, our reality. And this must lead us, inspire us, and motivate us into action, action that will help us to build something new, something freer, something that allows each one of us to live the life that God has given, in the way God intended; that is the freedom of which the Bible speaks.[49]

There are many important points in Sra. Flores's statement. The women are approaching the Bible with *their* questions. They do not reject outright what they hear from the pulpits, but their experience tells them that what they hear may not be answering their questions or supporting their liberation. They not only pose the questions but they also aim to answer them in their work and in ongoing theological reflection.

SEA's regular meetings for theological reflection and discussion often invite someone to facilitate the discussion, such as a nun, priest, or a worker in another barrio. Through these groups, they become their own interlocutors in these settings and keep their focus on the experiences of the poor in their community. This helps to assure that the outcome of their theological reflection is cognizant of, and cohesive with, the community.

For these women and for their community, the Bible stands as a unique source for inspiration and comfort, and as an encouragement to challenge nonliberative structures. Despite the fact that the Spanish brought the Bible at the same time that they indentured indigenous Peruvians, the women speak freely of the church they both share and do not share with those who conquered their land. As María Ramos Vega states:

> In the Bible, we can experience a real sense of God's presence with us. Jesus was poor. We are poor. Jesus was marginalized. We are marginalized. Jesus changed things for the better and this is what we are trying to do. If you read the Bible carefully, Jesus was never trying to take advantage of others. We see that the Spanish came here with two goals: they wanted to conquer our country and they wanted to spread Christianity. Through our communal reflection, we understand that the two do not go together. They are opposites. So now, we are trying to build something new; something that we discover for real in the Bible.[50]

There is also a sense that the Bible relates to the disparate narratives of multicultural El Agustino. Scripture is not used solely to assuage the sense of alienation or suffering. Through their Scripture study in SEA and in the numerous base communities throughout El Agustino, biblical narratives are frequently used as historical examples of the same oppression and marginalization they experience. Sra. Montes López said: "Our goal is not to make everything fine with our Biblical reflection. No, we want to grab the bad experiences we have had and bring them right to the top. The important thing is that we take the power out of those negative experiences by searching the Bible for similar stories."[51] With the decrease in the influence of negative experiences comes an increase in the critique of existing power structures in the community. "We can be very suspicious at times," stated Sra. Ronquillo Peña, coordinator of the Women's Team. "You would be surprised at the number of organizations that have approached SEA offering help, and then we find out that they have an ulterior motive."[52] This process of diminishing the power from the negative experiences means seeing the reign of God as possible, at least partially, in their own time. This results in a dialogic relationship between the biblical narratives and the reality of the barrio, which fosters a healthy hermeneutics of suspicion regarding some of its Christian heritage.[53] This, in turn, encourages the development of something new—a more intimate knowledge of Scripture, structures that will assist in building a society in which freedom is, the unifying of the people, and a grounding in the faith are realized.

The format of SEA's biblical reflections begins with the women asked to take the time to read and reflect upon a passage. For example, a topic at one reflection was Mary Magdalene in Matt. 27–28.[54] The passage is read out loud two or three times. This particular discussion began with an exploration of the belief handed down through the centuries that Mary Magdalene was a reformed prostitute. The women explored the texts for evidence of this accusation. They became aware of the historical distortion in this regard and proceeded to discuss how this same situation had affected their own lives.

"When I first started working for SEA," said Sra. Centano Salazar, "the men in my neighborhood were making comments to my husband that I was 'out of control' and he would probably lose me. There were jokes made that I was having an affair when I worked in the evening."[55] Several of the other women related similar experiences connected with the start of their volunteer or paid work.

The women then discussed how this distortion of Mary Magdalene's story had reduced her to a sexual being and diminished the power of a woman's witness. This insight was considered in the context of El Agustino and SEA. They related some of the barriers they face simply because they are women. Without bitterness, the women explored the implications of a woman who was going against societal norms and experiencing the diminution of her work and dedication. Of particular importance for the women was that Mary Magdalene was one of the biblical women who stood by Jesus in his time of need. Celia Sánchez Rojas mentioned that "the idea of Mary is so important to us because there are times when we feel we are standing alone at the base of the cross. We look up and sometimes feel that everything we have worked for has been for nothing. But we too need the courage to go ahead to the tomb."[56]

Equally essential to their interpretation was that Mary Magdalene delivered the good news of Jesus' resurrection to the other apostles. The women of SEA prayed about this in their own context and asked for the strength, wisdom, courage, and perseverance that Mary Magdalene exhibited in her life. They see her as a living example of faithfulness, leadership, and spirit, as well as a close friend of Jesus Christ. Sra. Montes López, who was facilitating this group, commented, "If we do not have a sense that we are on a mission, I think we would soon lose our ability to move ahead. But if we keep foremost in our minds the message of Jesus Christ, we can survive and thrive and continue to bring the good news to the people of El Agustino."[57]

Without much use of critical or outside resources,[58] the women explore the texts in-depth and consistently incorporate the issues of their own lives into their interpretation. Their intelligence, perception, and life experiences allow them to articulate what is often hidden or subjugated in the text. Their courage permits them to explore texts that are often overlooked in the missionary legacy of their country. In this way the Bible becomes a "dangerous" resource—dangerous in the sense of the recovery and activation of that which many in the church and society would prefer to remain fallow. The women realize that they possess the intelligence and perceptiveness to interpret the Bible on their own. As Relinda Sosa Perez stated:

> I was brought up in the Catholic church believing that everything I needed to know about God came from the priest. Not even the nuns in my elementary school discussed the Bible with us. Therefore, I never made the stories of the Bible personal until I came to work for SEA. We now openly approach any text we want. And we have discovered what an endless source of strength and consolation the Bible can be.[59]

Their expansive knowledge, perceptive interpretation, and deep love for the Bible are inspiring for all Christians. Indeed, if Christians individually and the church collectively are intent on taking the side of the poor, it is essential that we also listen to their biblical interpretations and join with them in their exploration.

Jesus in Latin America

The implantation of a Spanish image of God remains powerful in the minds of the people. Here God is the judging, demanding Father whose focus is very much on life after death—an image that suggests that suffering is the true path to holiness. Yet the theological development of the women places them in a process of healing that entails an evolution of the face of God.

More often than not when they speak of God, the women relate their images, sensations, and stories of Jesus Christ in their lives. Jesus remains foremost in their minds because it is here they discover a living example of someone like them—someone who struggled to correct wrongs, sacrificed to build anew, loved in order to heal.

The image of a demanding God the Father replaced by yet another image of a male may seem incongruous or confusing at best. However, as Sra. Torres said,

> We live in a society where many of the men in our lives, our fathers, brothers, uncles, and husbands, have treated us with

> disdain, and this is what we came to expect. But to see Jesus both as a male and as someone who loves us, respects us, and supports us means that we can start to see those same traits in men.
>
> When I was a child, my mother taught me to obey and respect the men in my life. I was too young to understand it at the time, but now I realize that what she was teaching me was how to survive. I no longer need to survive in that way and I look to Jesus to help me.[60]

As the image of the critical God the Father fades, the reality of a compassionate Jesus emerges. However, the shift in image does not stop there. Here is a realization that the image of God presented by priests, nuns, mothers, and fathers, was not complete. In a society that remains essentially male dominated, the appropriation of the loving, yet still challenging, Jesus into their lives permits a reinterpretation of the idea of maleness and its role in society. In turn, the women at times have successfully challenged the men in their lives to change. This step from submission to a deeper understanding of the mutual responsibility of male/female relationships is illustrated by Sra. Bravo:

> I was married at 16 and had my first child nine months later. At the time, my daughter and I were completely dependent on my husband for everything. I thought this was the way it was supposed to be because this was how my parents lived. Each day my father would give my mother just enough money to buy what we needed to eat that day.
>
> When I became involved in the *comedor*, suddenly I was the one who was the provider for others who had less than me. At first, I did not really understand the change but then my husband lost his job and I became the provider at home, too. Slowly I began to realize that it should not be a situation of him or me but of us together. This came to me when we heard the story of the loaves and fishes at Mass. Everyone there shared and I began to understand the message of Jesus in a new way. He calls each one of us to share in the same way—husbands and wives, workers and bosses, sisters and brothers, friends and neighbors. My husband has changed because of this but I do not think that would have happened if I had not been working at the *comedor* and listening to Jesus speak to me.[61]

Several of the women spoke of their identification with Jesus due to their sense of affinity with what he did in the first century C.E. "Can't you see it?" asked Sra. Castillo Reyes. "Can't you see Jesus walking in and joining one of our meetings? Jesus is not always on the cross for me. No, Jesus is right here working with us. He is one of us."[62]

Sra. Castillo Reyes and others affirm the transcendental nature of Jesus Christ as well as the universality of his praxis and message. In their identification with the person of Jesus Christ, they also express their desire for the same type of personal relationship he has with God, the ability to imitate Christ in building the reign of God, as well as the living out of the trust and faith he exhibited. The christological meaning of Jesus' service to others is brought alive in their work.

The full Christian faith of the women merges the orthodoxy and orthopraxis that is the focus of theological writing.[63] While speaking of and considering Jesus as a friend, they also maintain the divinity of Christ in their hearts and words. In this sense, they undergo a continual process of conversion that brings them closer to the Gospel of Jesus Christ and makes the Gospel live in El Agustino. Their faith is rooted in a deepening understanding of Christian tradition that is anything but otherworldly. This faith and understanding shows itself in their concern for the poor and for their work for justice from a woman's perspective.

A Transforming Mission

Consejo Episcopal Latinoamericano (Latin American Bishops Council or CELAM) in Medellín, Colombia, in 1968 included this depiction in its final report:

> Latin America is obviously under the sign of transformation and development; a transformation that, besides taking place with extraordinary speed, has come to touch and influence every level of human activity, from the economic to the religious.
>
> This indicates that we are on the threshold of a new epoch in this history of Latin America. It appears to be a time of zeal for full emancipation, of liberation from every form of servitude, of personal maturity and of collective integration. In these signs, we perceive the first indications of the painful birth of a new civilization.[64]

Now, over three decades later, one cannot help but be encouraged and disheartened—encouraged because great strides have been taken in realizing this vision of liberty for humanity; discouraged due to the many forces that are still working against the possibility of people living their lives fully. In the process of working toward an improvement of the El

Agustino context, the women are rediscovering and strengthening their faith. In their critique of the social structures that plague the people, they are acquiring an enthusiasm that brings their work alive.

There are many reasons for these transformations. First, the journey is a deeply spiritual one for these women. The ordinary, and extraordinary, circumstances of their lives have compelled them to deal with contexts they might never have imagined. For example, many of them came from situations where their primary concern was the feeding of their own families each day. This often involved herculean efforts in their early days in the barrio. Little could they imagine that one day they would be responsible for cooperative kitchens that feed tens of thousands of people daily. In addition, they recognize that this providing of sustenance often means the difference between life and death.

The scope and vision of the women have been amplified in many ways. They discovered that their God is the God of life and that their involvement in the promotion of life is indispensable to their faith. Likewise, they understand that the oppression they and their neighbors suffer is incompatible with the message of Jesus Christ. From concrete circumstances including homelessness, hunger, disease, and alienation, they realize that how they live their lives and live their faith are inseparable. As Zenaida Zúñiga Medina said,

> If you had told me that my faith would increase by my dealing with the very thing I was trying to avoid, poverty, I would have told you that you were *loco*. What has happened is that I have come to see the face of Jesus in many of the people for whom I work. Even the terrible ones. Now tell me what I should think about that. God's work is not always easy to understand.[65]

Second, the aspirations of the women have also affected and challenged the local church. In their individual way of interpreting the Gospel, they have brought alive the Gospel message in ways that the church in El Agustino and elsewhere in Peru have not always succeeded in doing. As they became agents of their own change, agents rooted in Gospel values, the people and the clergy of El Agustino have learned to turn to the women for inspiration and support. In other words, in their living out of the Gospel, they read the signs of the times for others. They make known that the God that they and their neighbors worship does not create or condone the inhumanity they experience.

Third, they understand that their position as women does not mean a role of subservience but rather one of leadership and change. This personal development occurred in the process of their work, their exploration of God's word, and their reflection. It was not something that remained within the group but has an influence on many women for whom they labor. By their example, they are able to challenge age-old concepts of womanhood and provide living manifestation of viable and productive alternatives. Their lives are examples to many women, particularly the young, as they successfully live out alternatives to traditional roles.

Fourth, for themselves and for those with whom they work, the women have been able to lift up the concept of being poor and to instill it with dignity and worthiness. In their conscious decision not to flee El Agustino at the first possible opportunity, they declare both their dedication to the people of the barrio and their assertion that poverty itself is no disgrace. In their bearing witness to the uplifting of the poor, they undergo a change of heart and provide the same opportunity for their friends and neighbors. This necessitates bearing witness in their words and deeds to Jesus Christ and to his teachings. This also requires their intimate understanding of the roots of poverty and the actions required to eradicate it.

Fifth, in the fecund, controversial, troubled, and yet creative environment of El Agustino, the women rise up to meet the challenges of the times. While doing so they live out a way of doing theology exemplified by Jesus Christ. Granted, they have little recourse to the theologies of the Northern Hemisphere except in their interaction with various nuns and priests. However, the paradigm they provide can inspire new paths for other theologies. Theirs is one way of faith seeking understanding. Their theology demonstrates the importance of examining the faith of the majority of the world and receiving the gifts of these rich resources.

Faith, Justice, and God in Concrete Situations

The testimonies of the women of El Agustino reflect the participation of women as they assist many of the over 152,000 people who inhabit its hills. Their words also reveal the impact of women's participation in the promotion of life and in making a change for the better. As community leaders, mothers, and wives, they are examples of the commitment of faith and solidarity with the poor.

Theologian Karl Rahner, S.J. wrote of the human person being radically open to the transcendent, oriented to the mystery we call God. Through the gift of free will, human persons may transcend themselves and in the search for meaning come to understand more of their own being and orientation. The search for meaning reveals the ineffability of life yet also hints at its meaningfulness. And Rahner argues that the revelation of God is invariably historically mediated. God must be encountered always yet partially in the here and now. In the human search for meaning, the path leads to an examination of one's history, present, as well as the one's hopes, dreams, and imaginations of the future. In Rahner's method, is the absolute necessity of the free subject who may exist as an "exemplar" of God's presence.[66]

In El Agustino, we find a living, concrete working out of the historically mediated revelation of God. *Servicios Educativos El Agustino* was founded to promote sustainable development in the barrio, promote leadership in the popular sectors, and do so with an eye to the Gospel. In other words, their goal was to make actual the Gospel in their community—the Gospel that calls each human to live a life of dignity, never to live with the lack of basic needs. As SEA matures, it is apparent that it has positively touched the lives of thousands. Interaction with the organization has promoted dignity, provided opportunity for personal growth, and has been integral in the preservation of life. Three SEA projects have been instrumental in creating positive changes—three projects that are "exemplars" of God's presence.

The Projects

Las MIADES

The creation of the *Micro-Areas de Desarrollo* (Small Areas of Development or MIADES) in El Agustino was one of the most important steps in which SEA has been involved.[67] From 1987 to the present,[68] the MIADES were instrumental in creating social order, coordinating municipal action, and developing self-government. Prior to the establishment of MIADES, there was not one coordinating body for the many organizations (e.g., the *comedores; Vaso de Leche* (Glass of Milk [Children's Food Program]); the *Federación de Mercados* (Public Markets Federation); and the *Asociación de Industrias en Desarrollo de El Agustino* (El Agustino Association of Industries in Development) that worked for the people in the barrio. The influence of the collective energies of these groups was not tapped.

When the *Izquierda Unida* (United Left Political Party) was successful in the 1983 elections, this signified a substantial change in the dynamics of the barrio. Local municipal governments regained and increased their power and the priorities of the neighborhood became the prerogative of the local municipality. For a short time, the municipal government of El Agustino was able to make some improvements. The electoral victory of *Aprista* (*Alianza Popular Revolucionario Americana*, Popular Revolutionary American Alliance or APRA) in 1986 resulted in the reduction of public works and the dismantling of the *Comisión de Saneamiento Físico-*

Legal (Sanitation Commission or COSFIL). The public works of the latter were crucial to the reduction of disease in the barrio.

In the meantime, architect and urban planner Jorge Acosta proposed the creation of three *Zonas de Tratamiento Especial* (Zones of Special Treatment or ZTE) for the areas of El Agustino that suffered the worst urban problems. The biggest problems he identified were sewage in gutters, lack of clean water and electricity, and the scarcity of jobs. Sadly, density was not a consideration although two- and three-room buildings without indoor plumbing housing more than twenty people were not uncommon.

Each micro-area was to have the following elements that would promote economic and urban development: unified production; an infrastructure between zones that would guarantee the existence of a local market; as much unskilled labor as possible; the availability of material necessary for the creation of jobs; and the existence of public services such as garbage collection, functioning sewage removal, and electricity.

To sell the idea, SEA organized meetings with all of the other NGOs in El Agustino as well as with community leaders. These evolved into meetings in every district of the barrio for the general population. "Without the influence and support of SEA, this crucial first step would never have taken place," said Francisco Chamberlain, S.J.

> Just walking through the neighborhoods, you would never realize the extensive network of grassroots organizations that exist. I believe that this is cultural in many ways. What we see here is the cooperative and communal mentality of the *campesinos* [peasant farmers] somehow translated into the urban environment. When you consider the fundamental, vital aspects of life, these are areas that put you into association with others. However, all of this was torn asunder by the move to the city, the daily struggle to survive, the terrorism, and the deep-rooted sense that they had no control whatsoever over their lives. This is where the women stepped in. In reality, they have always been the ones who have kept the family, specifically, and society, in general, together. Here, they made it possible to resurrect that sense of cooperation that most people thought had been lost forever.[69]

SEA organized a collective of the various groups in El Agustino that then was able to put pressure upon the Lima city government. With the financial support of the city, the MIADES were created and SEA provided the training for various groups to diagnose and prioritize the problems. This culminated in the first *Plan de Desarrollo Distrital* (District Development Plan).

In the intervening years, the political machinery of Lima has attempted repeatedly to dismantle the MIADES to centralize all power in the city government or to place priorities elsewhere. However, due to the strength of the organizations in El Agustino as well as the financial independence of the MIADES, the latter have survived and made a substantial change in the welfare of the community.

La Educación Popular

After SEA's founding in 1978, its first emphasis was the relocation of the new immigrants, basic services, training programs to prepare people for jobs in the urban environment, and motivating the residents to participate in development programs.[70] In the late 1970s and early 1980s, a new dynamic began to mark life in the barrio. It was then that the women of El Agustino began actively to organize and operate new programs. The women were responsible for developing training programs in carpentry, metalworking, masonry, and other skills. These programs were primarily for the men of the district because, as Sra. Montes López said, "There existed a deeply psychological debilitation among the men of the barrio due to their inability to support their families. Many of them came from the countryside where their primary activity was farming."[71]

Additionally, the women reached out in the capacity of advisers to various neighborhood groups in order to expedite the development of social service programs. These included the *comités de Vaso de Leche*, *comedores*, as well as programs for children. The women recognized that the people, especially the women of the district, were anxious to help but lacked the leadership skills necessary to implement popular organizing. This situation resulted in new levels of organization within SEA in order to train leaders to respond to the needs of the community.

In the following years, SEA underwent ongoing analyses of its goals and concluded that it must be a center of popular education for the barrio, as its name implies. This was to be their point of entry into the community. The subsequent development of programs meant training people to be leaders, spokespersons, and motivators in the life of the barrio, city, and country. The role of accompanying the people and their organizations is a noted characteristic of SEA. This means not coming in to solve a problem as experts but working with the people toward a solution. Accompanying had, and still has, the goal of helping people confront injustices and fully assume their responsibilities as citizens of the country. The women of SEA labor so that the people may come to realize the importance and righteousness of their desires and work. The intention of its programs is to empower and reaffirm *el actor popular* (best translated as "the community organizer"). SEA projects are continually reevaluated to ensure that they may be self-propagating.

SEA is indisputably rooted in the community of El Agustino. Sra. Ronquillo Peña said,

> Our approach is a *circuito metodológico* (circuit methodology). The Latin root of the word "education" refers to an action of construction as a guided process for others. In SEA, our intent is to provide education that is constructive in connection with the historical identity of the people. Our educational activities have as their end the allowing of each resident of El Agustino to be more of a person, to be valued, loved, and to be able to realize the "I" they are as well as the "we" we all are together.[72]

There is no expectation on the part of the women that they create identities but rather that they create the structures in which individual identities may flourish. Srta. Ronquillo Peña went on to say,

> The other idea of the etymology of the word "education" is guiding. Education has to be a process that guides the people to be educated and then to become educators. The search for the truth, the path to follow, is a task that implicates everyone. The last point is important because we recognize that no one person is the possessor of the whole truth. The search is always an ongoing task, is always in front of you. The educator may have more knowledge but this does not mean that the educator is more important in the process. The educator, in many aspects, fills the role of *provocador* (instigator or fomenter), a person who helps the people to come to realize the knowledge they already possess, and to use this knowledge as a means toward action.[73]

The women do not see themselves as a school nor do they have a predetermined schedule upon which the "educated" are free from the "educator." The process is fluid, and the goal is that the people for whom they work are never dependent upon them. The principal formulation of the *circuito metodológico* (methodological circuit) is what SEA calls ACAS—*acompañamiento* (accompaniment of the people), *capacitación* (encouraging individual and collective abilities), *asesoría* (assessing the problems), and *sistematización* (systemizing the tasks required to work toward solutions). This method was developed when SEA was newly founded and it has supported the programs and continued to evolve in the intervening years.[74]

El acompañamiento literally means to walk with another person. Colloquially, it means encouraging and provoking people and living in community. It is a process in which the "educator" does not place any distance between herself and the people. The process most often produces affection and friendship. In other words, there is an emphasis on personal relationships with the people and on being present in their daily lives. Entry into the lives of others presupposes an ongoing process that is always partial, always unfinished, and always rooted in respect for the autonomy of individuals and groups. The invitation from the people to enter into their lives is also integral, as is the accompaniment that the women leaders provide each other.

La capacitación signifies the enabling and empowerment that takes place in such moments as the *cursillos* (short courses), *encuentros* (meetings), and *jornadas* (workdays). What distinguishes their manner of *capacitación* is the relationship of these moments with the *acompañamiento* and *asesoría*. They understand that empowerment must take place before the accompaniment and the assessing process.

La asesoría is not simply the orientation and skills the women provide, but also the daily work, the ongoing dialogue with the people, the understanding of how to realize opportunities, and how to respond to the challenges the people face. The women state very clearly that they do not possess *las palabras magicas* (the magic words). Instead, it is one of those privileged moments for the affirmation of identity, capacity, and autonomy.

La sistematización implies the ordering of priorities. This encompasses the memory of the worker, evaluating one's life, achievements, and deficiencies, as well as delineating hopes for the future. These same steps are taken for the *sistematización* of groups. The questions that SEA poses in the process relate to the life experiences of the worker, the level of active participation, and what SEA could do to improve the process and the conditions.

These processes inherently involve both constant references to one's faith as well as a system that is new for most of the residents of El Agustino. This is the introduction of an economical dialectic distinct from the experiences of these former *campesinos*. This touches upon the rhythm of work, the way of making decisions, ways of proceeding in the urban environment, and participation in a democratic process. The educational challenges consist of the introduction of this dialectic and its appropriation by the people. Through these challenges comes a deeper understanding of the truth.

Las Organizaciones Economicas Populares

Economicas Populares refer to the collective activities carried out by the marginalized people to reduce the cost of living.[75] These would include all individual and group initiatives not instituted by the federal or municipal governments. In other words, this is the informal sector of the economy. There are an estimated 3,700 *micro-empresarios* (businesspeople operating small ventures), 4,000 *ambulantes* (street merchants), 80 *comedores*, and 550 *comités del Vaso de Leche* in El Agustino employing 80 percent of the district's workforce. Obviously, these are economic bodies that demand attention.

SEA delineates between two economic systems at work in the barrio: that of "survival" or *lógico de cosumo*, and that of "accumulation" or *lógica empresarial.* Margarita Córdova Herrera, the head of SEA's *Proyecto de los Bancos Comunales* (Communal Banks Project), describes the local economy in this way:

> The informal sector is the backbone of the economy in El Agustino. You must realize that the poverty here makes the area very unappealing to outside investors. Although we continue to work to have industry and commerce move to the barrio, it is an uphill battle. As usual, we are compelled to take matters into our own hands. This has meant the creation of various structures that will train a person for a job, provide seed money if that is necessary, and then provide ongoing analysis and assistance to the entrepreneur.[76]

SEA created the *Equipo de Proyectos Empresariales* (Business Projects Team) in 1990 to create employment opportunities as well as to act as income-producing sources for SEA. The women also have an ongoing concern about those areas that need attention and upon which they have not focused. As the number of people, particularly women, who were interested in establishing a business grew, SEA saw the need for "microcredit." The possibility of the general population of El Agustino qualifying for small business loans was negligible. Thus, the Communal Banks were formed.

SEA functions as a financial institution, offering savings accounts and capital for small business loans. The goals of the banks are to assist with credit applications, promote the concept of savings, provide up to a hundred dollars in seed money, and formally develop and train the women. There are currently thirteen communal banks in operation with over five hundred beneficiaries. Although men are not excluded, the emphasis is for women entrepreneurs because they are the majority interested in starting a small business.

The structures established by the women are not merely means for people to advance financially. Although financial improvement is part of the goal, equally important is creating an environment of self-worth, hope for the future, personal dignity, and self-sustaining systems.

Workshops

In their response to the needs of the people of El Agustino, the women of SEA develop and operate numerous workshops throughout the barrio. The topics are determined through consultation with neighborhood groups. In 1998, SEA ran more than eight hundred workshops throughout El Agustino, with topics including child nutrition, prenatal care, self-defense, financial management, small business start-up, gerontological issues, workers' rights, community organizing, and biblical reflection. Two workshops in particular, human rights and leadership training, are representative of what SEA works to accomplish.

Role of Education in Human Rights

A primary human rights focus of SEA and *La Coordinadora Nacional de Derechos Humanos* (National Coordinator of Human Rights or CNDDHH, of which SEA is a member) is the promotion of the rights of women. This was an inevitable decision on the part of both organizations as a consequence of various circumstances: the terrorist situation (that resulted in the deaths or imprisonment of thousands of men, nationwide displacement, and women forced to assume the role of family head and provider); the widespread violence against women; forced sterilization; and the fact that the majority of unschooled people in Peru are women.[77]

During the height of the terrorist era, the government of Peru focused almost solely on countering the internal disruption of the country. The question of human rights was virtually abandoned as insurgent forces were systematically disrupting essential services and kidnapping and murdering citizens. Peru became a country in which displacement, disappearance, and death were conditions distressingly familiar.

The women of SEA instituted a series of workshops throughout the barrio with the following objectives in mind: educating people about basic human rights, explaining avenues of recourse, obtaining free legal aid, and mounting protests to the government that are coordinated with CNDDHH. Due to the need to speak publicly about these concerns, the women trained others (many of whom have little or no education) to address ongoing violations and their causes. "Whenever I get scared or overwhelmed," said Rosa Pacheco, "I just think of Jesus chasing the money changers out of the temple."[78]

The Move from Volunteer to Administrator

The second most illustrative example is the leadership training workshops. The majority of women who now have paid positions at SEA began their tenure as volunteers. The organization has a policy through which leaders are identified and offered the possibility of additional training to assume administrative positions there or elsewhere. "Through this process," said Sra. Montes López, "we have been able to 'graduate' dozens of women on to paid positions in NGOs throughout the barrio.

> Our training involves two components that make moving up in SEA or out into another NGO applicable: our focus on the human nature of our work and our ongoing emphasis on bringing the Gospel alive. We do not mind providing training that leads people elsewhere because of our emphasis on building good community. To form this community we must first create a strong band of socially minded individuals who have the capacity to encourage human development, especially that which involves quality of life.[79]

In the training process, the need still exists for SEA staff to remember that they are one of the people. The women see this as key to guaranteeing that the desires and needs come from below and not from administrators. In the years since the founding of SEA, many women have said *yo ya no soy la misma opa de antes* (I am not the same dummy as before). *Opa* is a Quechua word. This statement reveals the long road so many of the women must travel in order to develop a sense of self-worth.

The instruction a woman receives also prepares her to deal with domestic difficulties that often arise after she starts working outside of the home. Many of the women were expected to maintain the same level of housework and food preparation that existed before their outside jobs. "This is an ongoing problem," said Benedicta Serrano Agüero, "because Peruvian men would never think of shopping, cleaning, or cooking even if they were out of work and their wife was the sole source of income."[80] At times like this, the women sometimes ask one of their husbands to meet with the recalcitrant spouse. The women are also trained in domestic confrontation skills. A side effect of this process is the change of attitude on the part of many sons and daughters. All family members stand to learn about the fragile equilibrium necessary to maintain a balance at home. "That is why," said Sra. Montes López, "we are also very active in the mental health area. You quickly realize that home, work, friendships, faith, and church are all closely interrelated."[81]

SEA Finances

The growth of SEA has been organic in that it has responded to immediate issues first. These issues initially meant the resettlement of thousands of people in the barrio, organizing food availability, interfacing with the constantly changing political machinery of the city, and developing educational programs. As SEA grew, it became obvious that new sources of income were necessary. *Caritas de Dinamarca* (Caritas of Denmark, a Catholic agency for overseas aid and development)[82] and the *La Virgen de Nazaret* parish provided the original funding for SEA. After the *Equipo de Proyectos Empresariales* was formed, a bakery, a restaurant, and a food store were created to function as income-generating sources, as places of employment, and as locations where people were able to obtain inexpensive, nutritious food. Additionally, the organization conducts fund raising activities in Lima and solicits donations from abroad as well. In the past several years, foundations in the United States, Germany, France, and Spain have made grants ranging from US$5,000 to US$100,000. After *directora* (director) Sra. Montes López and activist Benedicta Serrano Agüero traveled to the United States to receive awards and deliver speeches, several individuals from the audiences stepped forward to provide ongoing donations.

A Narrative, Listening, Acting Theology

Most of what we have heard thus far comes from the narratives of the women of El Agustino. In the telling of their stories—their tales of success and defeat, connection and separation, faith and skepticism, and amazement and disappointment—they come to a greater understanding of themselves and of their faith and of their God. This is a rekindling of the manner in which we first discover our faith in the stories of the Bible. The process continues as the women uncover the manner in which the biblical stories relate to and inspire their own stories. In this fashion, they are able to lift up their personal narratives, quite often out of the mire of their sociohistorical situation, so that they might reflect the transcendence of God in their own time.

Who the women are, the faith they possess, the manner in which they respond to God, and the understanding of God that develops, are all the yield of what makes up their narrative, individually and in community.

Because they are willing to share their stories with each other and with outsiders, they contribute to the ongoing quest for a comprehension of the divine. In their personalization of Scripture, they show that the mere knowing or memorization of Bible passages is insufficient. Moreover, they challenge those with whom they have contact to do the same—integrate the biblical narrative into their own. They do not contend that their narratives in conjunction with the Bible are a sole or exclusive source of theology. They do live out, nevertheless, the conviction that this is a source not to be overlooked.

The foundation of the women's theology is found in the fact that they do engage Scripture in a dialogical relationship with their historical circumstances. In this way, the women see the saving action of God both in the Bible and in their lives. God's redemptive acts then become a continuous path throughout history and are literally alive and tangible.

One crucial element that has been underplayed in narrative theology, however, is that necessity of careful listening. It is impossible to enter into the listening process as a tabula rasa. Nevertheless, great efforts must be made to assure that the listening process has a beginning and middle of solely listening. If interpretation is to occur as soon as one hears the words expressed in narrative form, one runs the grave risk of imposing meaning on them that may be incongruous with their intent. Obviously, explication at any point is fraught with this problem, both for the speaker and for the listener.

A final step that helps to attest to the validity of the words and interpretations is the examination of the actions that back up the words. Clearly, if there exists a discrepancy between what is spoken and how the speaker lives, the validity of any interpretation is jeopardized. The possibility of such a discrepancy in the case of the women of SEA is minimal. This is due to the consistent attention paid to their personal stories and to their biblical reflections within the organization and in the community, which act as a check and balance for the individual in her theological quest.

Confronting Demons and Idols

The precarious nature of life in El Agustino is obvious. However, facts and statistics may even lead to the depersonalization of the circumstances and the immunity of the outside viewer to this reality. One must then turn to the suffering faces of the poor: the child whose mental capacity has been permanently damaged due to preventable malnutrition; the young woman whose life of child-bearing has already destroyed her health and whose husband has destroyed all sense of self-worth; the worker who acquiesces to illegally low wages and long hours to be able to take anything home; and the elderly person who has witnessed the disintegration of familial support and who has subsequently lost hope for the future.

These are the faces that the women encounter each day. Sadly, the number of issues with which they contend could fill volumes. Therefore, I want to highlight the following two to exemplify the response of the women.

Domestic Violence

Violence is a subject that has personally touched the lives of each of the women in one or more forms—terrorist, criminal, or domestic. In whatever form it is experienced, it exists in direct contrast to the covenant they have with their Creator. "When I have a headache or I am anxious about missing a deadline," said María Ramos Vega, a volunteer at *comedores populares* and at *Vaso de Leche*, "I do not equate this with the suffering that is inflicted upon a woman by her husband or boyfriend.

> But we have been given this gift from God and we are all called to protect and enhance it in whatever ways we can. I have witnessed the far-reaching effects of a man striking a woman. Her sense of self-worth goes down and with it her ability to face life's obstacles. Instead of promoting her own life and the lives of her children, she is forced to resort to surviving as well as she can. Her children then see this as the way they are to live their lives—as abusers or as the abused.
>
> When we were visiting an abused woman in her home once, her husband came in and he told us to go "do your Christian things." It was not the time for me to say this but I wanted to say, "I am doing my 'Christian thing.' I may not be able to change the husband, but I may be able to change the way the wife thinks."[83]

In their struggle to work against the negative forces present in their surroundings, the women accept their responsibility in the creational process. One of the women names herself a *partera* (midwife) in this regard. The domestic violence does not remain within the sphere of statistics, fractured bones, or broken homes. It is identified as a sin and dealt with accordingly. "The Holy Father has spoken of the "culture of death," said Elena Decheco, a freelance writer and volunteer at SEA, "I understand the emphasis on matters such as abortions and euthanasia. But what must also be understood is that the victim of domestic violence is being killed just as if someone were slowly and repeatedly putting a knife in her. All possibility of her life being full of promise slowly drains away."[84] Sofía Macher, Ph.D., the executive secretary of CNDDHH indicated, "80 percent of the demand for intervention from local human rights groups originates in family violence issues."[85] In 1993, the last year for which statistics are available, the *Delegación de Mujeres de la Capital* (Women's Capital Delegation) registered over five thousand acts of life-threatening violence against women in Peru.[86] Underreporting sets this around one tenth of the actual number. The lack of reporting may be attributed to several factors: shame, lack of recourse available, retribution, neglect on the part of Peruvian society, and the sad resignation by many women that this is an intrinsic element of married life.

Domestic violence scars the entire family. Self-esteem is torn down, fear is inculcated, girls come to accept this as normal, and boys learn to perpetuate this violation by example. It must be noted, too, that abuse vitiates the transgressor.

The examination of the presence of domestic violence is immensely complicated. One must take into consideration the upbringing of all parties, the presence of alcohol or drugs,[87] issues of subjection and submission, the sense of inferiority, and the inherited societal image of women as well as that promoted by modern advertising. Peruvian society carries the implicit and explicit message of women's inferiority. "Women here receive the message from birth that they are at the service of men," stated Carmen Lora, Ph.D., a professor at the PUC and administrator of the *Instituto Bartolomé de Las Casas*. "Poor women usually lack any possible role model to counteract this indoctrination."[88] Paradoxically, it is often the woman in a poor family who preserves the unity of the family.

Domestic violence was among the most pressing problems when SEA was first organized. As Sra. Castillo Reyes states, "As creatures of God, we must be accountable for our own behavior as well as responsible for creation as it exists where we live. We work very hard at SEA to preserve life but we also accept the responsibility of promoting the dignity of life."[89] The women candidly acknowledge the debilitating effects of domestic violence as well as the Christian call to promote the abundant unfolding of life in their midst.

Religion and the Market

The women of SEA are familiar with the papal encyclical *Rerum Novarum* (*On Capital and Labor*, Pope Leo XIII, 15 May 1891) and its criticism of capitalism. In a capitalist country in which a majority of the people struggle to meet their most basic needs, they understand the shortcomings of this economic system. They have also read and reflected upon John Paul II's more recent encyclicals *Laborem Exercens* (*On Human*

Work, Pope John Paul II, 14 September 1981) and *Centesimus Annus* (*On the 100th Anniverary of Rerum Novarum*, Pope John Paul II, 01 May 1991). Their appreciation of these and similar documents is rooted in their belief that human salvation takes place in the midst of creation and not in a privatized, spiritualized space. The uninterrupted confrontation with life and death circumstances leaves them no other option. Consequently, their theological reflections often take the form of determining if a particular system, program, or development works for or against the eschatological promise. As these women run communal banks, training programs, communal kitchens that feed thousands, and interact with government, ecclesiastical, and international authorities, there is little that is naive or uninformed about their analysis. As Christians, administrators, and local theologians, they are well-qualified to make critical analysis of their context.

"Hardly a week goes by when someone does not ask us if what we do is really Catholic," said Sra. Montes López.

> Some people feel that we have stepped out of the boundaries of propriety for women in our work. However, the Christian nature of this work is a good question to ask ourselves. Look, we have learned that there is nothing in our environment that is abstract or merely theoretical. Our faith calls us, demands for us to evaluate the world around us. Although our world is never black and white, the extremes that we experience here in Lima allow us to see clearly if something leads to or away from God. In a country with so much poverty, this frequently focuses on economic issues. We do pray over Matt. 6:24[90] and recognize that two masters cannot be served. On the other hand, we are fully aware of the necessity of money in order to solve so many of our problems. Therefore, there is always some tension between the need for money and the need not to be controlled by money or to obtain it through means that are rooted in exploitation.[91]

The women are also aware of the situations that are more difficult to judge. They speak of their work with people who have subsequently cheated or robbed them. They mention those who literally have been saved from starvation and homelessness only to flee the barrio at the first opportunity. They readily see the positive effects of capitalism but from a distance—few of these benefits "trickle down" to El Agustino.

In their study of Catholic social teaching, they have developed the ability to analyze economic systems in Peru and to determine both the negative and positive repercussions. A market economy that provides income with dignity is their aim. However, they also are attentive to those economic machinations that continue to exploit the most vulnerable and work to change them. For example, the city government's attempt to remove *ambulantes* from the streets is instigated by what is considered to be the *ambulantes*' negative impact on tourism. It has little to do with a desire to improve the marketability of their goods. Therefore, SEA has actively worked to protect the street merchants as well as provide new economic structures through projects including MIADES.

The strategies developed by the women to implement change have been inspired in part by John Paul II's encyclical *Centesimus Annus*. In fact, the women commented that the letter appeared to have been written with El Agustino specifically in mind. The encyclical deserves quotation at length because its applicability is obvious:

> The fact is that many people, perhaps the majority today, do not have the means which would enable them to take their place in an effective and humanly dignified way within a productive system in which work is truly central. They have no possibility of acquiring the basic knowledge that would enable them to express their creativity and develop their potential. They have no way of entering the network of knowledge and intercommunication which would allow them to see their qualities appreciated and utilized. Thus, if not actually exploited, they are to a great extent marginalized; economic development takes place over their heads, so to speak, when it does not actually reduce the already narrow scope of their old subsistence economies. They are unable to compete against the goods which are produced in ways which are new and which properly respond to needs, needs which they had previously been accustomed to meeting through traditional forms of organization. Allured by the dazzle of an opulence which is beyond their reach, and at the same time driven by necessity, these people crowd the cities of the Third World where they are often without cultural roots, and where they are exposed to situations of violent uncertainty, without the possibility of becoming integrated. Their dignity is not acknowledged in any real way, and sometimes there are even attempts to eliminate them from history through coercive forms of demographic control which are contrary to human dignity.
>
> Many other people, while not completely marginalized, live in situations in which the struggle for a bare minimum is uppermost. These are situations in which the rules of the earliest period of capitalism still flourish in conditions of

> "ruthlessness" in no way inferior to the darkest moments of the first phase of industrialization. . . . In spite of the great changes which have taken place in the more advanced societies, the human inadequacies of capitalism and the resulting domination of things over people are far from disappearing. In fact, for the poor, to the lack of material goods has been added a lack of knowledge and training, which prevents them from escaping their state of humiliating subjection.[92]

Many of the projects and workshops just discussed directly address the deliberation of the encyclical on the lack of skills and knowledge necessary for the poor to advance. Similarly, the respect for, and abetting of, the multiple cultural traditions found in the barrio help to alleviate the "violent uncertainty" that is extant in El Agustino. Having overcome numerous attempts to remove the people from the land or to force them out through the lack of basic services, the women of SEA continue to struggle for the uplifting of the dignity of life. Communal kitchens and banks, while seemingly small in the overall scheme of El Agustino, have both combated the subjection inflicted upon the people and proven that alternative economic systems are viable. Here we witness directly the impact of globalization as well as the effort to diminish its negative effects.

Utopian Vision

The words of the women reveal a conviction that what exists now can and will be changed for the better. Their vision of a better place is eschatological due to the inherent connection they perceive between what they are doing now to build the reign of God and how they will experience the reign in the future. Their unremitting focus on the present historical situation makes it clear that their utopian vision begins with their earthly reality. "We see almost every day," said Sra. Montes López, "the little improvements that take place in our lives. Of course, there are setbacks. But faith allows us to take these in stride."[93]

SEA began its operation with programs to solve the most pressing problems of the barrio. Gradually, as the women solved problems and became more expert and confident in their work, a shift occurred. They were no longer just solving the emergencies they faced in a particular day but they were analyzing the sources of the problems to eradicate them for the future. As a necessary part of this process, their web of connections expanded to include municipal and federal governments, political parties, experts at local universities, foreign specialists, as well as international foundations. The development and modification of their methodology enabled them not only to analyze the problems but also to use this analysis to condemn publicly the origins of these problems. The women and their neighbors were thrust into the public space as they met with government and private industry officials. The poor, who had been ignored for centuries, now had well-informed voices proclaiming their needs and condemning the conditions that perpetuate their state of being.

At SEA, the women continue to create and sustain programs that will not only assist the people but also inform them of the distinct possibility of bettering their lives—as long as they get involved. The response, as noted in the success of their various workshops and organizations, was an impetus to move forward. As they and the people they serve were able to imagine improvements, the effects of the hermeneutical spiral spread throughout the community. As each step in the process of creating programs was achieved, the level of awareness of the unacceptability of the situation in El Agustino was raised.

The subversive memories of the women are operative here as, in fact, any utopian vision must be subversive. The idealization of the time ahead necessarily entails changes. In the case of El Agustino, the changes demanded are prodigious and require action that will subvert the status quo. The memories of the women are retrieved and intensified as the creation of something better transpires. The process of rejecting the current conditions entails the imagining of that which is better.

"We often feel inspired not just by our successes," stated Sra. Mejia, "but also by the thoughts of what could possibly be."[94] These "thoughts of what could possibly be" have thrust the women into challenging, imaginative, dynamic, and spiritual circumstances in which sinful structures are identified as just that and alternatives arise from faith-filled consideration of the call of God. This also entails on the part of the women a willingness—indeed, a freedom—to enter situations previously unimagined. "Perhaps the reason we spend so much time reflecting on the Bible," recalled Sra. Centano, "is that at times what is happening is so frightening that we only have God's grace to depend on."[95] Their faith, coupled with their willingness to undertake risk, reaches beyond their current state, sustains their commitment to their neighbors, and constructs a future that allows for the creation of a new idea of humanity.

The women must confront such questions as what freedom means—for what are they struggling to be free to do? At the same time, what is this new humanity? These questions plunge them into the consideration of the dynamics of the psychological, the interrelationship with other humans, as well as the manner in which they handle their successes and defeats. The individual and complex visions of the time ahead must be balanced with those of the community where they live. As Sra. Cáceres said, "We are challenged constantly to ask ourselves if and how we are connected to God in the life and example of Jesus Christ. This is not an easy task because it is very personal and it is extremely difficult to describe. However, without this constant checking, we can flounder."[96] Through their concrete actions in the community, they and other residents of the barrio are able to evaluate the direction in which they move. Their faith allows them to proceed and their theology permits an intelligent, coherent articulation of their faith. Yet, as Leonardo Boff, O.F.M., indicates:

> Faith does more. Faith is not concerned only with a religious and theological reading and elucidation of reality. . . . Faith not only passes judgment on the utopia of others; it develops its own utopia for person and society. With it own versatile brush and rich palette, faith paints a picture of the future. Here the incarnation of God in Jesus Christ—his life, his historical projection of liberation, his violent death, his resurrection, and the consequent presence of the Holy Spirit in our history—are the cardinal elements of the positive side, the utopian side. In terms of the vision of faith: to what, when all is said and done, are we called?[97]

To answer Boff's inquiry, I turn to the words of Esther Arteago Serrano, the coordinator of the Children's Movement:

> I have learned from my mother to keep my eye on the world around me and on a future, a future I will never completely understand. But this is where I learn about God. This is the only way I have. So here I am rooted in the earth, in the barrio, but I keep my eye on something ahead that is grander than I can imagine. That is God and that is what I am headed for.[98]

Conclusion

Starting with the often stark reality of their lives, what was important was understanding and using the suffering they and their neighbors endure, employing Scripture to personify their struggles in light of the Gospel, realizing that words are useless if they do not incite action, and discerning that lives hanging in the balance are the utmost cause to which they must respond. A thread woven throughout all of this is the recognition of a God to whom they are called to respond and a vision of something better toward which they work. Inherent is the God who revealed Godself in the work, words, cross, and resurrection of Jesus Christ. In this divine revelation, they discover what informs every symbol they experience and every doctrine they follow.

While they may not speak the terms of creation, redemption, eschatology, sacrament, and revelation, their personal words and actions reveal these mysteries of the faith. The women do not argue that their theology encompasses all of the great symbols of the Christian tradition.

Yet, here is the gift that must not be overlooked. In their reality exists an understanding of Christ as the revelation of God and of whom we are all commanded and empowered to become. The women themselves understand this command and experience this empowerment. And they work to allow others to do the same. Together they promote the awareness of the way in which God's identity as love motivates their quest for a more complete understanding of God. Together they recognize in Jesus Christ God the origin, sustainer, and end of all reality—and they actively and fruitfully advance their agency in the project of God's creation.

Recipients of grants of $100 from SEA's communal banks,
allowing them to start small businesses in the barrio

CHAPTER 5

The Path Ahead

Changes in Community/Changes in Theology

Fifty years ago, El Agustino hardly existed. Today it is a community of over 152,000 people. This *pueblo joven* (young town), like so many throughout the city of Lima and throughout the country of Peru, has been the site of a sociological phenomenon as multiple cultures, languages, and religious traditions unite to form community. Theologically, this barrio demands a new approach due to its unique nature. As Robert J. Schreiter writes, "whether one begins with the context and moves to theology, or one begins with the theology and moves to the context, changes in context have to be taken into account by theology."[1]

El Agustino is touched by a constantly changing array of influences: globalization, terrorism, church, machismo attitudes, internal migration, and poverty. The barrio is in a state of flux and the signs of the times demand to be constantly reread and reinterpreted. This, in turn, presents us with questions that must be answered and tasks that need to be accomplished when faith seeks understanding.

The Questions

The women of El Agustino suggested two important questions in various ways. One of these, reproductive rights, involves the freeing of women from the cultural norm of viewing themselves primarily in the role of motherhood. If we look toward that time when all people, to use the words of Iranaeus, a second-century bishop, give glory to God when fully alive, motherhood will undoubtedly play an important role for many women in Peruvian society. However, when a woman's role is envisioned solely as mother, while at the same time most poor mothers are compelled to work to support a family, the conflict between social expectations and necessity diminish the possibility of being fully alive.

Second, the image of God is undergoing changes in places such as El Agustino. Due to their continual theological reflection, the women of SEA are discerning the presence of God in ways that do not always reflect the thinking or wishes of the mainstream church. It is important to see how their image of God is developing and how this motivates and changes the focus of their work.

Reproductive Rights

> *It is contradictory to be in favor of women's rights and not be in favor of women's reproductive rights. This is a very hard knot. The question of reproductive rights has alienated so many women from the church. How do you explain to the mother of ten that she cannot use any form of birth control although she can barely feed the children she has now? The patriarchal attitudes of the church prevent the bishops and priests from addressing this dilemma and from hearing the voices of women all over the world.*
>
> *Also, as a woman's awareness of herself increases, she begins to see herself in terms other than just motherhood and* ama de casa *(housewife). What we witness here in Peru is a woman using birth control, trying to remain faithful to her church, and yet experiencing debilitating anxiety and guilt over her decision. If a woman's role is to bear children continually, she will encounter tremendous hurdles.*
>
> Maryknoll Sister Rosa Dominga Trapasso
> Director,
> Center of Creativity and Change

Human reproduction was seldom discussed in the interviews except by educated administrators and secular feminists. However, using birth control, other than natural family planning methods, is commonly admonished from pulpits. The issue is complicated by an inherent desire on the part of many women not to make this a public conversation—in their family, community, or parish.

The sentiments of Rosa Dominga Trapasso were reiterated by Soraya Ronquillo Peña, Ph.D., the coordinator of the Women's Team, who stated, "one of the constant problems we face is the lack of resources. This is made worse by families that have ten or twelve children. We are a Catholic organization and we will not go against church rules. However, we do offer natural family planning workshops, but even these are not supported by the Archdiocese."[2] The complexity of the situation was illustrated by Benedicta "Beni" Serrano Agüero, the executive director of the School of Leaders of the Central Federation of *Comedores Populares* Lima and Callao, who said,

> Right now there is a big argument going on between the church and the government regarding birth control. However, this . . . consists of a lot of men talking to a lot of men and no one is asking the women how we feel. This is manipulation by people who really do not understand what is going on. I ask myself, "Why is there not a space in which we women can say what we want and not have these decisions made by the government or the church?" Is ignoring half of the world's population Christian?[3]

The church has continued to protest the inclusion of family planning programs in the *Ministerio de Promoción de la Mujer y del Desarrollo Humano* (the Ministry of Promotion of Women and Human Development or PROMUDEH).[4] Clearly, the question of family planning is not unique to Peru but one that is at the forefront of numerous conflicts in the Third and First World. The topic of abortion was discussed occasionally but the primary issue is the prevention of conception in the first place. The image of women in Peru is still identified with the domestic tasks of childbearing, shopping, cooking, and cleaning. However, 59 percent of the women in Lima also work full time.[5] The number would approach 80 percent if part-time and at-home businesses (e.g., sewing, assembly work, etc.) were included.[6]

The societal expectation that woman should bear and raise children, maintain a household, and work to support a family is untenable at best. This expectation does not acknowledge the toll that such a burden takes on the family. It also hinders the possibility of a woman being able to develop herself and her skills. If a change is going to take place, however, it must begin with the poor women of Peru because they are the ones most gravely affected. Birth control is readily available to the upper classes and the stigma of using it does not carry the same weight, as is the case in most countries. However, due to the cultural Catholicism so instrumental among the poor, the stigma of using birth control is significant.

The question remains, What are the women of SEA to do about reproductive rights for the poor women in the barrio? Some light is shed on the situation by the words of Sra. Ronquillo Peña:

> We see our task in the area of reproductive rights to be threefold: first, we must continue to educate the women of the barrio that their womanhood is not limited to motherhood. In many ways, we have made great strides but it is a very complicated issue. Poor Peruvian women see their role primarily in this capacity. However, the inability of the family to support numerous children has opened new avenues of consideration. With most mothers being forced to work at least part time, even the men are beginning to see the unsound aspects of numerous children. As we train more women to take their dignified place in the marketplace, the women understand that other possibilities exist.
>
> Second, we have applied for and received more grants to operate natural family planning clinics. This is an ongoing problem because many women are still reticent about discussing what they consider too personal a situation. However, as we increase our network throughout the barrio, it is possible to provide more information on this option.
>
> Third, small groups have been formed to discuss this issue and what may be done in regard to the church's decision on family planning. Although we do not hold great hope for a change soon, we have been able to reach out to many of the priests and nuns in the barrio. I doubt that we will hear the warnings against all forms of family planning that occurred in the past.[7]

The simple change of attitude on the part of the women in El Agustino instigated by conversations, workshops, and printed material has brought the topic of birth control to the forefront. Gradually, changes in attitude are occurring—changes that will have far-reaching effects as women, particularly poor women, throughout the world undergo a rise in consciousness on the issue of reproductive rights. Slowly, the restrictions against the full participation of women in social and church settings will be lessened as patriarchal attitudes continue to be challenged. Eventually, even if the family-planning policies of the church are slow in occurring, the ignominy of birth control will be lessened.

Our God or Their God?

The image of Almighty God the Father brought to the continent by Spanish missionaries was more judgmental than loving, more condemning than forgiving, an image that served the purposes of the Spanish conquerors as it facilitated their imposition of an Iberian form of order and control. Not all of the early missionaries were ill intentioned. Sixteenth-century Dominican priest Bartolomé de Las Casas is perhaps the best-known example of those who determinedly defended the humanity and dignity of the indigenous population. He spent a lifetime challenging the church and the empire. Nevertheless, there is a sad history of injustices inflicted upon the people of Peru in the name of God and church.

History shows that the forbidding God handed down by the Spaniards and others is losing its efficacy in the imaginations of the people of El Agustino. One hears more of a God leading one to a righteous life in service of others in a place where service is so essential to survival. As Relinda Sosa Perez, a coordinator of neighborhood *comedores* (communal dining rooms), said,

> When we experience fulfillment that overcomes the sense of not belonging, when we understand that the Spirit leads us on and at times we will not understand the path, when we realize that it is in the midst of the poor and powerless that we experience God, there is no need for an judging image of God. Perhaps the people of power need the image of a powerful God but we not only know weakness intimately, but we have come to see God living in the weakness with us.[8]

There is no doubt that God is intricately woven into the fabric of Peruvian society. Yet there are aspects of this presence in which God may be misidentified with the church. For instance, members of the church hierarchy are guaranteed to be as present at political and social gatherings as any other group. Newspapers daily feature stories of the activities of the hierarchy. New homes and businesses are regularly visited by members of the clergy for blessings.

In the current ecclesiastical environment of Peru, the European connections are particularly held in a place of honor. Loyalty to Rome is highly valued. The social agenda of the church in Peru, so prominent in the tenure of Cardinal Landázuri, is tabled by the current archbishop. He stated in his installation homily:

> We know, remembering the words of the Holy Father John Paul II, that the Christian faith does not intend to fit in a rigid plan to change the sociopolitical reality and it recognizes that the life of man develops in history in imperfect and diverse conditions. The Church, therefore, upon ratifying constantly the transcendent dignity of the person, utilizes its own method with respect to liberty.[9]

Many of the women of SEA were there for the archbishop's installation and they left the liturgy with two predominant thoughts, as expressed by Ofelia Montes López, the director of SEA:

> The archbishop's words left us feeling as though we were told that our work was not important and not part of the agenda of the church. Support from the archdiocese has decreased over recent years and we assume that this trend will continue. Truthfully, we are disappointed and discouraged.
>
> On the other hand, we have been disappointed many times in the past but we have also discovered that new challenges often lead us to reconsider our work for the better. It is hard to imagine that God does not approve of the feeding of the hungry, the clothing of the naked, the freeing of those who have been imprisoned in a life of want. When the archbishop says that the church has its own method regarding liberty, I do not think that he is speaking of liberty in the same sense that we are. But I would like to remind him that we are the church too; we are the body of Christ.[10]

Tension exists between the church represented by the hierarchy today in Peru and by the church that exists among Peru's impoverished masses. Just as the early missionaries were often unwilling to enter into the lives of the conquered people and into their relationship with their gods, today there a sense that what the hierarchy represents as the real church is viewed as distinctly European. As Gloria Apaza Cruz, a buyer for a *comedor* cooperative, states:

> My grandfather used to tell us stories that had been handed down through his family (of Quechua-speaking, Incan descendent people). He was a very devout man in the Catholic Church but he also used to ask us, "Did the missionaries think that for hundreds of years our people never thought about God, that we never loved, that we never struggled?" He would teach us that we were God's people before the Spaniards arrived and that we must never think that wisdom only came with the missionaries.[11]

In a country that has been the birthplace of far-reaching theological thought, it seems that the current hierarchy desires the return of the church in Peru to the thinking of another era when all that was valuable in theological thought came from above and not from the people. This stands in stark contrast to the biblical theology from which the Christian faith grew. The move backward represents a disregard for the essential involvement of all God's creatures in the ongoing and incomplete move toward the reign of God. The current trend indicates a diminishment of the ever-present incarnational work of God.

The conquerors of Peru used power to overcome the active resistance of the people. Power is again being inappropriately applied in an attempt to create uniformity—uniformity that stifles the recognition of the call of God to God's people. After surviving obstacles and demons, after hearing and responding to God in novel and sometimes controversial ways, after being lifted up not only out of dire circumstances but also up toward a more intimate relationship with their God, these women are not about to be deterred by hierarchical preferences that appear to thwart their journey.

The Road Ahead

My observations lead me to conclude that there are fruitful avenues to explore that could enhance the work of the women and provide direction for people elsewhere in Peru, Latin America, and throughout the world.

First, there is the question of the relationship between the women of Peru and its liberation theologians. While the methodology of liberation theology has been employed by other theologies (also named liberation) throughout the world, little has been done regarding women in the birthplace of this theological school. Part of the reason for this may be attributed to the lack of trained women theologians in Peru. However, the foundation for this school came from the poor and it can continue to do so.

Second, the relationship between the work of secular feminists and poor women in Peru offers great possibilities for mutual assistance and advancements. In conversations with both groups, it was apparent that they work toward many of the same goals.

Third, the women of El Agustino, by virtue of what they have done and plan to do, represent a future direction for liberation theology—that is, practical efforts on the local scene.

Association with Liberation Theology

Latin American liberation theologians were censured by the Vatican, declared insignificant after the fall of the socialist state by some theologians and social scientists, and criticized for their lack of attention to the issue of women in church and society by North American feminists. One may wonder if this school has a future or if it will be considered merely a theological trend that has come and gone. Gutiérrez said, "I was a Christian before I was a liberation theologian and I will be a Christian if liberation theology no longer thrives. Theologies are born to die. The important thing is not the name but the absolutely essential focus on the problems of the poor."[12]

Liberation theology may never again attract the attention it received in the past three decades but, as theologian Ian Linden wrote, "The fundamental tenets of liberation theology (have)—almost surreptitiously—been broadly accepted in many part of the Catholic Church."[13] The basic tenet of this school, "a way to understand the grace and salvation of Jesus in the context of the present and from the situation of the poor,"[14] is more pressing today than ever before. The world is, if possible, more difficult to understand than when the first liberation theologians started to write in the late 1960s. The model for understanding our world has changed. Our ideas of what it means to be human, who our God is, and how we are interrelated are undergoing transformation as our world becomes more complex. And the increase in complexity may be verified by the fact that the problems addressed by the earliest liberation theologians are worse today.

The themes of liberation theology have expanded to include the questions of gender,[15] race,[16] popular religion,[17] the environment,[18] political theology,[19] other nations,[20] as well as other religions.[21] Having expanded out of its birthplace in the Third World, this school may now be discovered at all levels of education, in theological reflection groups, popular education, and community organizing. The far-reaching effects of liberation theology cannot be ignored or dismissed.

Before the death knell of liberation theology is tolled, the experience of women in Peru must be considered. Specific steps might accelerate the momentum that the women are building. The *Instituto Bartolomé de Las Casas*, the primary liberation theology research institute in the world, is still an active theological force in Peru and throughout Latin America. It may fall to the women of SEA to increase the connection with the institute. From their voices will continue to come new interpretations of Scripture, examples of faith to embolden others, encouragement for those struggling for the poor, and a cry that may break through the deafness of those who live more comfortably. There are many insights that may take more than just a listening to their words. The wisdom of the women is often experienced more than just heard. While these women may be unaccustomed to speaking academic theological language, they are familiar with responding to the call of God in ways that reveal their souls and psyches.

Building a Relationship with Secular Feminism

Some of the women working at SEA expressed a sense of distance from secular feminism, often due to its staunch support of reproductive freedom for women. Certain women at SEA have connections with organizations such as *Centro de la Mujer Peruana Flora Tristan* (Flora Tristan Peruvian Woman's Center) and *Movimiento Manuela Ramos* (Manuela Ramos ["everywoman"] Movement), the two primary feminist institutes in Peru. However, they indicate that they usually do not speak of these at work. On the other hand, most of the women at the two feminist organizations, according to María Emma Mannarelli, Ph.D., a staff member at Flora Tristan, are practicing Catholics. Dra. Mannarelli has lamented the fact that secular feminists have so little to do with poor women and with their projects.

When one considers the primary foci of the feminist centers—investigating and reporting on the oppression of women in Peruvian society, supporting women's citizenship and autonomy, promoting women's rights at home and work, as well as producing academic research on the history and sociology of Peruvian women—it is obvious that their goals are harmonious with those of SEA. It may take the outreach of the women of SEA to bring the women of SEA together with the wealthier, more educated women of secular feminism. Clearly, the two groups have much to offer to one another.

Not the Time for Grand Visions

When liberation theology emerged in the late 1960s, it profoundly touched a chord in people around the world. At that time, there were many who foresaw the future of the church in the theological developments that were emerging first from Peru and then from increasingly large numbers of theologians throughout the world. Due to the profound and extensive reception given to this school by students and theologians, great things were expected. Without doubt, this school has implemented untold positive changes in the thinking and action of the world's believers. Nevertheless, perhaps the sights were set too high and some came to be disappointed in the eventual outcome.

The success of the women of El Agustino has been, and continues to be, a result of the fact that they remain local. With the conscientious decision to remain in the barrio, they focus their lives and energies on their neighbors and friends. By remaining local, they are able to achieve results in part because they work in an environment with which they are intimately acquainted.

All theologies throughout history have been the product of a particular set of historical and social contexts. A theology's success or longevity is dependent upon the *sensus fidelium* (sense of the faithful). By nature, however, longevity is not a concern of the women of SEA. The tasks that they have identified and to which they have committed themselves are immediate. Their dreams and imaginations take them sometimes beyond the boundaries of the barrio. However, they recognize *la llamada de Dios* (the call of God) in the concrete here and now of El Agustino. With limited resources but seemingly limitless faith, they continue to build the reign of God. Their desire, as expressed in various ways, is to remain in the barrio because of their deeply rooted connections, their knowledge of the barrio, as well as the sense that this is where God is calling them to be.

Liberation theology addressed huge problems over the past three decades. Most of the questions faced in the last century, however, remain with us: poverty, violence, hunger, homelessness, and the lack of dignity. Today, numerous local movements continue to fight against injustice throughout Latin America and throughout the world. They have the ability to be attuned to the new questions, issues, and concerns demanded by a quest for justice. The path forward may exist within local movements such as SEA that have the capacity to listen carefully.

A Different Liberation

The reader familiar with feminist and liberation theologies will observe many similarities between those and the theology emerging from the women of El Agustino. On the other hand, the desires of the women, their work, their theological reflections, as well their daily habits, expose important differences that call for examination. Although the process of faith seeking understanding, the doing of theology anywhere in the world, interacts more with the poor today, it is still not a common path. Yet it is the voices of the poor, and here I speak especially of the women, which call for recognition, for healing, for sustenance, and for justice—voices that insist on action. From these voices arise the call to implement change. There can be little doubt that these voices are a major challenge across the disciplines. This challenge has put a face on the anonymous numbers of the poor and converted statistics into suffering human beings throughout the world.

The emphasis on the role that impoverished women play in this development is slowly changing the character of theology. It is not possible to do theology today without consideration of half of the population of the earth. The issue of gender is gradually taking its rightful place as voices that were forgotten, or to which were never listened, are being heard and the subsequent insights are being studied. As Zenaida Zúñiga Medina, a board member of the Central Federation of *Comedores Populares of Lima and Callao*, states, "the experience of us women is different. We struggle with the words but we know that the way we feel is very important to the way we think. Many men do not understand this."[22]

The women both love their church as well as criticize it for the ecclesiocentric dismissal that offers lip service while aiming to restrict their influence and overlook their wisdom. They recognize that their church exists in the flesh in El Agustino, and it is here that they will implement changes to work toward an inclusive ecclesiology. Necessity breeds change. Necessity has been a source of transformation in the church throughout its history. In the context of their struggles for justice on behalf of their neighbors, the women point out the need to change anachronistic church policies. In hearts that are strong and compassionate, they live out the words of *Lumen Gentium* (Dogmatic Constitution of the Church, 1964) that missioned the church to be "a sign and instrument of communion with God and of unity among all humankind."

The 1971 Synod of Bishops declared that "action on behalf of justice and participation in the transformation of the world fully appear as a constitutive dimension of the preaching of the Gospel, or, in other words, of the Church's mission for the redemption of the human race from every oppressive situation."[23] One may ask why, over three decades after this was written, the poor of Latin America are in worse straits. The answer is painfully obvious. These good words have remained just words for many. Small groups of people, such as the women of El Agustino, give life to the words—enflesh them and make them real.

It is also clear from the bishops' declaration that the Gospel itself remains just words without the living out of the Gospel. Some still argue that the promotion of justice erroneously impels the church into the political arena. However, the bishops also write that "The Church has the right, indeed the duty, to proclaim justice on the social, national, and international level and to denounce instances of injustice."[24]

To fulfill this duty of proclaiming the good news requires risks and it is this uncertainty that the women of this study have undertaken admirably. The theological foundation for these endeavors is easy to uncover. Fr. Gutiérrez used the Books of Exodus and Isaiah to reveal a God who is intimately involved in leading the people to freedom. Christian Scripture unmistakably tells us that God is love and that God may be found in the actuality of justice. This is not a presence that is perceived from just words but one that is found in the concrete actions and struggles for freedom, justice, and love. The Bishops encapsulated this when they wrote

> . . . love demands an absolute demand for justice, namely a recognition of the dignity and rights of one's neighbors. Justice attains its inner fullness only in love. Because every person is truly a visible image of the invisible God and a sibling of Christ, the Christian finds in every person God himself and God's absolute demand for justice and love.[25]

The bishops do not write of a suggestion or proposal but rather of the very demand that is integral to the life of every Christian.

The *koinonia* (community) that the church is called to build finds new architects in women like those who labor in mercy and love for justice in El Agustino. And this new way of being differs from a male perception. As integral as the Bible is to their work and reflection, the women refuse to accept those texts that reinforce patriarchy or machismo. Their competence in reformulating the idea of biblical authority emerges from the daily experience of life and death necessities.

Leonardo Boff writes: "Theology as regulated knowledge has its own mode of considering all things, that is, in the light of God. Thus, all things possess a theological dimension in that everything can be seen in reference to God or contemplated as coming from God. In this sense, as a perspective and a vision, theology is one."[26] Sra. Zúñiga elaborates Boff's sentiments:

> Look, you say that we women are theologians. I do not really know what that means.
>
> But I will tell you this: if being a theologian means listening to and reading the word of God; if being a theologian means trying to find God in all the *basura* (garbage) here in the barrio; if being a theologian means trying to understand how it is we can build the kingdom of God, then I guess we are.[27]

Sra. Zúñiga indicates that knowledge of faith is intellectual as well as existential. The mystery of God exists in every person as truly a visible image of the invisible God.

The church is the foundation from which these women set forth, as would be the case for any theologian, and they recognize the body of Christ in their neighbors and friends. Their faith, however, sometimes takes them on paths that diverge from those of the hierarchical church. And their theology is worked out in the realm of the *depositum fidei* (deposit of faith) as well as in the strikingly original and difficult environment of their community. The knowledge of these Christian people demands that they take into account their lives, their own history, *la llamada de Dios*, and the journey upon which this call takes them. The language of their theology is unconditionally human—that is, it speaks to and from human experience to unfold the Christian mysteries. This language addresses and accentuates the catechetical dimensions of their theology. Their search for truth becomes a steadfastly evolving experience that leads them beyond the printed facts into a rich and fruitful enlightenment.

St. Paul wrote, "The only thing that counts is faith expressing itself through love" (Gal. 5:6b). These women bring this alive through their categorical acts of love and their reflections on the faith of their church.

This way of doing theology brings forth the quintessential needs of their particular context. In the same way, it makes incarnate the God who saves; the God who hears the cry of the poor. Instead of destitution and distress emerging as irresoluble dilemmas, they become hermeneutical tools with which the women unfold the mysteries of the body of Christ.

Seeking to understand faith from the position of marginalization opens up the historical presence of impoverished, yet spiritual and loving, people. This presence amplifies theological reflection due to its intimate knowledge of the church as mediator of revelation. Questions predominate the theology of these women more than apologetics. Nevertheless, the theological agenda of the oppressed arises from the majority of God's people, from their silence, from their disappointments and their joys, and from their accomplishments. Herein we witness the beginning phases of a theology and a new humanity.

Women and Future Theological Discourse

From their lived experiences, the women of El Agustino have developed a Christian language about God; they have formed a theology. They indicate through their work and reflection how talk of God can be very practical. In relating their own experiences to the stories of the Bible, they pursue our oldest means of understanding God—living stories of beginnings filled with hope, tales of failure and setback, narratives filled with faith and joy, as well as suffering and persecution. In these stories—of the Bible and in El Agustino—we discover an authentic language about God. We discover the active subjects of theology and faith. They possess the authority of the faithful.

From the perspective of women here and elsewhere, we may experience new and unique proclamations of the Christian faith. They are the spokespersons not for individuals but for the collective enterprises in which they are involved. Beyond that, women are spokespersons for humanity, as men have always been. They symbolize life in the here and now because they repudiate the denigration of the everyday tasks that occupy the time of all humanity. Rather, they lift up the ordinary as a true sign of God's incarnation in our midst. Because they are not closed to the ordinary or the new, they are capable of bringing forth novel, creative, and imaginative ideas. Their ability to keep their aspirations and desires in the forefront differs dramatically from a mode of thinking rooted in rationality and scientific methodologies. This seems logical when seeking understanding of God who is equated with love.

Many of the women of SEA spent a large part of their lives as, to use their words, *just housewives*. From this beginning, they have empowered themselves to recognize the life-giving nature of food preparation, child-bearing and raising, and care for others. They also have come to know that poverty may unite them with millions throughout the world, but it does not define them. They are women, poor, Christians, of various ethnicities, speaking several languages, married and single, widowed and divorced, parents or childless, educated and not. They have proposed challenges to the rest of the world that emerge from, but are hardly limited to, each of these descriptors. First world theologians stand to discover new ways of thinking if they sincerely ask what can be learned from the organic, local theologians such as the women of El Agustino.

If I were to venture one conclusion, it is this: What they have to say is what we must hear; what questions they pose, we all must toil to answer; what challenges they present, we must work together to meet.

Appendix: Interviewees

The Women of SEA

Edelmira Aclari Castellares
Home Province: Huancavelica
Position: Secretary of neighborhood school

Gloria Apaza Cruz
Home Province: Lima
Position: Buyer for *comedor* cooperative

Esther Arteago Serrano
Home Province: Lima
Position: Coordinator, Children's Movement

Gloria Bravo Palomeque
Home Province: El Agustino
Position: Sales Coordinator for the bakery

Irene Cáceres Sánchez
Home Province: El Agustino
Position: Founder and director of the first *comedor* in El Agustino

Rosa Canto Castro
Home Province: Huancayo
Position: Neighborhood coordinator, manager, *La Miel* restaurant

Rosa Castillo Reyes
Home Province: Lambeyeque
Position: President, *Club de Madres*

Modesta Centano Salazar
Home Province: Lima
Position: Secretary General, Town Council

Carmen Fernández Cano
Home Province: Santa Isabel
Position: Economic secretary for township

Paulina Flores de Osorio
Home Province: Ayacucho
Position: Founder of town of San Pedro (El Agustino), coordinator of *Clubes de Madres* and District Committee of *Vaso de Leche*

Lucy Mejia Calderón
Home Province: Ayanacuchana
Position: Coordinator of *comedores*

Rosa Pacheco
Home Province: Lima
Position: Coordinator, Federation of Women

María Ramos Vega
Home Province: Lima
Position: Coordinator at *comedores* and *Vaso de Leche*

Celia Sánchez Rojas
Home Province: San Martin
Position: Secretary General of township

Benedicta "Beni" Serrano Agüero
Home Province: Lima
Position: Executive Director, School of Leaders of the Central Federation of *Comedores Populares* of Lima and Callao

Relinda Sosa Perez
Home Province: Canta
Position: General Manager of neighborhood *comedor*

Elvira Torres Anas
Home Province: N/A
Position: Coordinator, National Center of Base Social Organizations

Martha Vera Belleza
Home Province: Ica
Position: General Manager of bakery, coordinator of *Vaso de Leche* committees

Zenaida Zúñiga Medina
Home Province: Apurímac
Position: Board member, Central Federation of *Comedores Populares* of Lima and Callao

SEA Staff Members

Margarita Córdova Herrera
Home Province: Lima
Position: Director, Communal Banks

Elena Decheco
Home Province: Moquegu
Position: Freelance writer, SEA volunteer

Ofelia Montes López
Home Province: Lima
Position: Director, SEA

Soraya Ronquillo Peña, Ph.D.
Home Province: Lima
Position: Coordinator, Women's Team; Dean, General Studies; and professor of social work at PUC

La Virgen de Nazaret Staff Members

Francisco Chamberlain, S.J.
Citizenship: El Perú
Position: Pastor

José Ignacio Mantecón, S.J.
Citizenship: Spain
Position: former pastor

Instituto Bartolomé de Las Casas Staff Members

Gustavo Gutiérrez, OP, Ph.D.
Home Province: Lima
Position: John Cardinal O'Hara Professor of Theology, University of Notre Dame

Carmen Lora, Ph.D.
Home Province: Lima
Position: Editor, *Páginas*; consultant to *Federación de Comedores Populares*

Luis Mejica, Ph.D.
Home Province: Ayacucho
Present Position: Coordinator of social studies programs at the

Instituto, professor of anthropology at PUC

PUC Faculty

Jeffrey Klaiber, S.J., Ph.D.
Citizenship: United States
Position: Professor of history

Imelda Vega-Centeno, Ph.D.
Home Province: Lima
Position: Professor, author

Secular Feminist Staff Members

María Emma Mannarelli, Ph.D.
Home Province: Lima
Position: Historian and board member, Flora Tristan Peruvian Woman's Center, professor of history at PUC

Liliana Ramirez
Home Province: Lima
Position: Financial Services, *Manuela Ramos*

Human Rights Staff Member

Sofia Macher, Ph.D.
Home Province: Ayacucho
Position: Executive Secretary, National Coordinator of Human Rights

Religious Women

Rosa Dominga Trapasso
Citizenship: United States
Position: Director, Center of Creativity and Change

Brigida Weiler, MMS, Ph.D.
Citizenship: Germany
Position: Coordinator of Social Services, *Callao*

Government

Miriam Schenone
Home Province: Lima
Position: former Minister of Promotion of Women and Human Development

Miscellaneous

Ricardo Antoncich, S.J.
Position: Professor, ESPFL (School of Pedagogy, Philosophy, and Letters)

Monseñor Luis Bambarén, S.J.
Position: Bishop of Chimbote, Peru

Jaime O'Leary, S.J.
Position: Principal, Fe y Alegría School, Jaen, Peru

A small business owner selling the crafts made by her family

Notes

Chapter 1

1. Rosa Pacheco, interview and translation by author, 06 March 1998, tape recording; *Servicos Educativos El Agustino* (Educational Services El Agustino or SEA), Lima.

2. See Cecilia Blondet, *Las Mujeres y El Poder: Una Historia de Villa El Salvador* (Lima: Instituto de Estudios Peruanos, 1991), 61–91.

3. For additional information on the life of Moyano, see Diana Miloslavich Tupac, *María Elena Moyano: En Busca de una Esperanza* (Lima: Centro de la Mujer Peruana Flora Tristan, 1993); and Jo Marie Burt and Aldo Panfichi, *Peru: Caught in the Crossfire* (Jefferson City, MO: Peru Peace Movement/USA, 1992).

4. Paulina Flores de Osorio, interview and translation by author, 03 February 1998, tape recording, SEA, Lima.

5. Rosa Dominga Trapasso, interview by author, 30 January 1998, tape recording, *Centro de Creatividad y Cambio* (Center of Creativity and Change), Lima.

6. Robert J. Schreiter, *The New Catholicity: Theology between the Global and the Local* (Maryknoll, NY: Orbis Books, 1997), 99.

7. Gustavo Gutiérrez, interview and translation by author, 25 February 1998, tape recording, Instituto Bartolomé de las Casas, Lima.

8. Gustavo Gutiérrez, *A Theology of Liberation*, trans. Sister Caridad Inda and John Eagleson, 15th anniversary ed. (Maryknoll, NY: Orbis Books, 1994).

9. Although there has been some criticism of the lack of consideration of the situation of women in Gutiérrez's theology [see *National Catholic Reporter* (Kansas, MO), 16 September 1996], Gutiérrez stated that

> I am working with and for *las señoras* now. But it is a complex question. I am not convinced that if I wrote something (about feminist theology and the situation of women) it would be new. I am not asking

> my friends in feminist theology to write a book about the problems here in Peru. Today, we have women theologians in Latin America who are working from this perspective. (Gustavo Gutiérrez, 25 February 1998)

10. Flora Tristan (1803–1884) was a French sociologist and feminist. Her book, *London Journal* (1840) contains an early and courageous defense of women's rights and labor reform. Her philosophy anticipates Friedrich Engel and Karl Marx. For more information on Flora Tristan, see Doris Beik and Paul Beik, *Flora Tristan, Utopian Feminist: Her Travel Diaries and Personal Crusade* (Indianapolis: Indiana University Press, 1993); and *Flora Tristan*, *The Worker's Union* (Chicago: University of Illinois Press, 1983).

11. María Emma Mannarelli, interview and translation by author, 01 April 1998, tape recording, Flora Tristan, Lima.

12. James B. Nickoloff, ed., *Gustavo Gutiérrez: Essential Writings: The Making of Modern Theology* (Minneapolis: Fortress Press, 1996), 17. Due to the previously unseen mixture of ethnicities existing in El Agustino, the consciousness-raising situation of which Nickoloff writes is a viable reality in the barrio.

13. Stephen B. Bevans, *Models of Contextual Theology*, ed. Schreiter (Maryknoll, NY: Orbis, 1998), 1.

14. Ibid.

15. Mexico Conference on "Doing Theology from Third World Women's Perspective," in *Feminist Theology from the Third World: A Reader*, Ursula King, ed. (Maryknoll, NY: Orbis Press, 1994), 41.

Chapter 2

1. The most thorough analysis of the *Aprista* Party and its cultural, religious, and political impact is Imelda Vega-Centeno B., *Aprismo Popular: Cultura, Religión y Política* (Lima: CISEPA, 1991).

2. Ibid., 99.

3. For a more complete history of Sendero Luminoso see Deborah Poole and Gerardo Rénique, *Peru: Time of Fear* (London: Latin American Bureau, 1992); David Scott Palmer, *The Shining Path of Peru* (New York: St. Martin's, 1992); Robin Kirk, *Untold Terror: Violence against Women in Peru's Armed Conflict* (New York: Human Rights Watch, 1998); Carlos Iván Degregori, *Que difícil es Ser Dios: Ideología y Violencia Politica en Sendero Luminoso* (Lima: Zorro de Abajo Ediciones, 1989); and Gustavo Gorriti Ellenbogen, *Sendero: Historia de la Guerra Milenaria en El Perú* (Lima: Editorial Apoyo, 1991).

4. See Jorge Castañeda, *Utopia Unarmed: The Latin American Left after the Cold War* (New York: Vintage Books, 1991).

5. The Armed Forces High Command of Peru announced on 18 July 1962 that the constitution has been suspended. The government was then under the direction of Gens. Ricardo Pérez Godoy, Nicolás Lindley López, and Pedro Vargas Prada, and Vice Adm. Francisco Torres Matos. This military government decreed reductions in support of education. See Degregori, *Que difícil es Ser Dios,* 8–12.

6. The fatalities from the war against Sendero Luminoso, including military, *senderistas* (members of Sendero), and civilians, rose from 170 in 1982 to 2,807 in 1983 and 4,319 in 1984. República Peruana, "Comisión Especial del Senado sobre las Causas de la Violencia y Alternativas de Pacificación en el Perú," *Violencia y Pacificación,* (Lima: DESCO y la Comisión Andina de Juristas, 1989), quoted in James D. Rudolph, *Peru: The Evolution of a Crisis* (Westport, CT: Praeger Publishers, 1992), 98.

7. An estimated 120,000 people from Ayacucho alone fled the department by 1986. See Billie Jean Isbell, "Shining Path and Peasant Responses in Rural Ayacucho," in *Shining Path of Peru,* 59.

8. Castañeda, *Utopia Unarmed,* 121.

9. See Gutiérrez, *Las Casas: In Search of the Poor of Jesus Christ*, trans. Robert R. Barr (Maryknoll, NY: Orbis Books, 1995), 11–44.

10. Luis Maza, "The Emergence and Development of *Sendero Luminoso* in Peru," *McNair Journal* (1994), 72. Also see Americas Watch, *Peru under Fire: Human Rights since the Return to Democracy* (New Haven, CT: Yale University Press, 1992).

11. "Guzmán defines Sendero's ideology as "Marxism-Leninism-Maoism-Gonzalo thought (*pensamiento Gonzalo).*" Castañeda, *Utopia Unarmed,* 119.

12. Joseph S. Tulchin and Gary Bland, eds. *Peru in Crisis: Dictatorship or Democracy?* (Boulder, CO: Lynne Rienner Publishers, 1994), 83.

13. Rudolph, *Peru,* 89.

14. U.S. Department of State. *Background Notes: Peru.* Bureau of Western Hemisphere Affairs <www.state.gov/www.background_notes/> (U.S. Department of State, 1999).

15. The unemployment figures can be misleading because they do not reflect those who may hold a job that pays less than a subsistence wage.

16. Americas Watch, *Peru under Fire,* 5.

17. Imelda Vega-Centeno, interview and translation by author, 19 February 1998, tape recording, Curia Provincial, Lima.

18. The imprisonment of Sendero's leadership came after Fujimori suspended the constitution, dissolved the Congress and the judiciary, placed several congressional leaders under house arrest, and imposed censorship of the press on 05 April 1992. See Tulchin and Bland, eds. *Peru in Crisis,* 5ff.

19. Francisco Chamberlain, S.J., interview by author, 16 February 1998, tape recording, Juniorado, Lima.

20. Gutiérrez, 13 April 1998.

21. For example, Quechua, the language imposed by the Incas upon the people they conquered, is spoken by an estimated 40 percent of the Peruvian population.

22. Jeffrey Klaiber, "The Church in Peru, Ecuador and Bolivia," in *The Church in Latin America: 1492–1992*, ed. Enrique Dussel (Maryknoll, NY: Orbis Books, 1992), 287.

23. The Archdiocese of Lima estimated that a million faithful pray before the image each year when it is processed through the city on its feast day, 13 November. Arquidiócesis de Lima, *Advocaciones y santos peruanos: Señor de los Milagros* (Arquidiócesis de Lima, 1999).

24. Rosa de Lima (1585–1617) was canonized by Clement X in 1671 as the first Latin American saint.

25. Martín de Porres (1579–1639) was beatified by Gregory XVI in 1837 and canonized by John XXIII in 1962.

26. Toribio de Mogrovejo (1538–1606) was canonized by Benedict XIII in 1726 and proclaimed patron-saint of the Latin American bishops by John Paul II in 1983.

27. Francisco Solano (1549–1610) was canonized by Benedict XIII in 1726. Other Peruvian beati and saints include Juan Masías, canonized by Paul VI in 1975 and Blessed Sor Ana de Los Ángeles Monteagudo, beatified by John Paul II in 1985.

28. Klaiber, "Church in Peru, Ecuador and Bolivia," 291. This trend has continued. In 1901, 82 percent of the clergy was Peruvian, a reversal of the previous century. However, by 1973, almost 62 percent of the priests were foreign born. Secretariado del Episcopado Peruano, "Iglesia en el Perú" (Lima: Secretariado del Episcopado Peruano, 1974), 11.

29. The Religious of the Sacred Heart arrived in 1848; the Jesuits were reestablished in 1871 after the order's suppression; the "National" Franciscans were founded in Peru in 1883; the Salesians arrived in 1891; the Congregation of Sacred Heart Fathers in 1893; the Sisters of the Reparation were founded for Peruvian women only in 1896; the Third Order Dominican Sisters (Teaching Dominicans) arrived in 1898; the Brothers of Mary (Marists) in 1909; the Brothers of La Salle and the Immaculate Heart of Mary Sisters in 1922; the Ursulines in 1936; the Dominicans of Saint Mary Magdalene in 1938; the Marianists in 1939; and the secular order, the Theresian Institute, in 1942. See Klaiber, *The Catholic Church in Peru, 1821–1985: A Social History* (Washington, DC: Catholic University of America Press, 1992), 144–164.

30. Ibid., 176.

31. George Foster, "Peasant Society and the Image of the Limited Good," *American Anthropologist* 67 (April 1965): 293–315.

32. For example, the following organizations were founded: The Center for Catholic Youth (founded in 1895 but reaching new strength in the 1930s); Fides Center (1930, appearing as a new group in 1944 and re-created in 1949 in conjunction with Catholic Action and UNEC, the student wing of Catholic Action); the Central Council of Women's Catholic Action (in Lima in 1931); and Women's Social Action (in Arequipa, also in 1931) both of which achieved great strides in the conscientization of women.

33. Two people in particular are of note: Victor Andrés Belaunde, who wrote the political classic, *La Realidad Nacional* (The National Reality), as a response to contemporary Marxist interpretations of Peruvian history; and José de la Riva-Agüero, whose two doctoral dissertations, *Carácter de la Literatura del Perú Independiente* (*The Character of Literature of Independent Peru*, 1905) and *La Historia en el Perú* (*History in Peru, 1910*) were intellectual staples. His very public return to Roman Catholicism and devotion to Catholic causes helped to combat the rampant anticlericalism in the oligarchy. Both of these men eventually taught at the PUC.

34. The principal organizer of the Mission was a laywoman, María Rosario Araoz, who was also instrumental in founding the *Oficina nacional de educación Católica* (National Office of Catholic Education or ONDEC) in 1955.

35. The parish of *La Virgen de Nazaret* in El Agustino still consists of a parish church and eight satellite chapels scattered throughout this barrio of more than 150,000 people. Two of the chapels date from this period.

36. See Secretaría General del Episcopado del Perú, "Primera Semana Social del Perú: Exigencies Sociales del Catolicismo en el Perú" (1959): 259.

37. The papers were succinctly entitled "Document on Justice," "Document on Peace," and "Document on the Poverty of the Church." See Alfred T. Hennelly, ed. *Liberation Theology: A Documentary History* (Maryknoll, NY: Orbis Books, 1990), 97–119.

38. Hennelly, *Liberation Theology*, 92–93.

39. Ivan Illich was born in Vienna 1926. He studied theology and philosophy at the Gregorian University in Rome and obtained a Ph.D. in history at the University of Salzburg. He came to the United States in 1951, where he served as assistant pastor in an Irish–Puerto Rican parish in New York. From 1956 to 1960, he was assigned as vice-rector to the Catholic University of Puerto Rico, where he organized an intensive Latin American culture training center for North American priests. Illich was cofounder of the widely known and controversial Center for Intercultural Documentation (CIDOC) in Cuernavaca, Mexico. Since 1964, he has directed research seminars in institutional alternatives in a technological society with a special focus on Latin America. He died in December 2002.

40. Illich, "The Seamy Side of Charity," *America* (21 January 1967), reprinted in Illich, "The Seamy Side of Charity," in *Roman Catholic Church in Modern Latin America*, ed. Karl Michael Schmitt (New York: Knopf, 1972), 152–163.

41. Dom Hélder Câmara, *Church and Colonialism*, trans. William McSweeney (Denville, NJ: Dimension Books, 1969), 111.

42. See in particular *Mater et Magistra*, John XXIII, *Pacem Terris*, John XXIII, and *Populorum Progressio*, Paul VI.

43. Bishop Bambarén, S.J., assisted by Fr. Ricardo Antoncich, S.J., headed the Commission. I am indebted to them both for the information in this section. See Luis Bambarén, S.J., interview and translation by author, 26 February 1997, tape recording, *Casa Nuestra Señora de Fátima*, Lima; and Ricardo Antoncich, S.J., interview and translation by author, 13 March 1998, tape recording, *Casa Nuestra Señora de Fátima*, Lima.

44. Luis Bambarén, S.J., 26 February 1997.

45. Cardinal Landázuri published a message in which he supported the expropriation of Standard Oil (which occurred a week after the takeover), but in the same message he called for elections and return to normal democracy. Klaiber, *Catholic Church in Peru*, 78. The agrarian reform of 1969, the Industrial Community Law of 1970, and the Property Enterprise Law of 1974 were all fully supported by the church. See Ricardo Antoncich, S.J., 13 March 1998.

46. Oficina Nacional de Educación Católica, "Centros educacionales dirigidos por religiosos: estudio de su distribución por diócesis" (Lima: Oficina Nacional de Educación Católica, 1971), 11.

47. Gutiérrez said, "When we first started to offer the summer course in 1971, there were only 75 or so participants. By 1985, we had over 2,000 and they came from everywhere: the teachers at schools, organizers in the *pueblos jóvenes* (young towns), priests, and nuns as well as the laity. Eventually people started to come from throughout Latin America and North America and Europe" (Gutiérrez, 25 February 1998.)

48. Alfonso López Trujillo was coadjutor archbishop of Medellín at the time. He would later become a moving force behind the attempt in the 1980s to discredit liberation theology.

49. Gutiérrez, 25 February 1998. He went on to say that

> The other liberation theologians, for example (José Míguez) Bonino (of Argentina), (Leonardo) Boff and (Hugo) Assman (both from Brazil), (Juan Luis) Segundo (of Uruguay), and (Jon) Sobrino (of El Salvador), and I were made to feel like *personae non gratae*. Although Trujillo and others tried to have us barred, we were invited as *periti* (advisers) for some of the more liberal bishops.

50. The cardinal was both the president of the Peruvian Episcopal conference and first vice president of *Consejo Episcopal Latino-Americano* (Latin American Bishops Council or CELAM) at that time.

51. See Hennelly, ed. *Liberation Theology*, 225–232.

52. Hanni Rolfes, mcs, *Nueva Evangelización: reflexiones, experiencias y testimonios desde El Perú*, ed. Francisco Rejón Moreno (Lima: Instituto Bartolomé de Las Casas-Rimac, 1992), 17–18.

53. Rosa Canto Castro, interview and translation by author, 18 February 1998, tape recording, SEA, Lima.

54. Hennelly, ed. *Liberation Theology*, 402. The complete text of this document may be found here.

55. A balanced and concise description of the use of Marxist analysis in theology may be found in Pedro Arrupe, S.J., "Marxist Analysis by Christians," in ibid., 307–313.

56. Enrique D. Dussel, "Theology of Liberation and Marxism," in *Mysterium Liberationis: Fundamental Concepts of Liberation Theology*, eds. Ignacio Ellacuría, S.J. and Jon Sobrino, S.J. (Maryknoll, NY: Orbis Books, 1993), 88–90.

57. In particular, see Hennelly, ed. *Liberation Theology*, 367–374 and 461–447.

58. Economist Dr. Saskia Sassen writes that

> economic globalization has reconfigured fundamental properties of the nation-state, notably territorially and sovereignty. There is an incipient unbundling of the exclusive territorially we have long associated with the nation-state. The most tragic instantiation of this unbundling is the global city, which operates as a partly denationalized platform for global capital. Sassen, *Globalization and Its Discontents* (New York: New Press, 1998), 81. Based upon her criteria, Lima is not a global city.

59. Schreiter, *New Catholicity*, 5.

60. G. B. Madison, *Globalization: Challenges and Opportunities* (Hamilton, Ontario: McMaster University Institute of Globalization and the Human Condition, 1998), 2.

61. Schreiter, *New Catholicity*, 13.

62. Teresa Valdes Echenique and Enrique Gomariz Moraga, eds. *Mujeres Latinoamericanas en Cifras* (Santiago: Facultad Latinoamericana de Ciencias Sociales, 1993), 21.

63. Castañeda, *Utopia Unarmed*, 125.

64. Valdes Echenique and Gomariz Moraga, eds. *Mujeres Latinoamericanas en Cifras*, 18. Also see Commercial Data International, *Country Review: Peru 1998/1999* (Houston: Commercial, 1999), 4–5, 18–27, 55–59.

65. See Michael L. Smith, "Shining Path's Urban Strategy: Ate Vitarte," in *The Shining Part of Peru*, ed. David Scott Palmer (New York: St. Martin's, 1992), 127–147.

66. Alberto Fujimori, who was named *el fenómeno Fujimori* (the Fujimori phenomenon) by the Peruvian press after his spectacular rise in the polls in the final three weeks of the 1990 campaign, defeated his opponent, novelist Mario Vargas Llosa, with 62.5 percent of the vote.

James D. Rudolph writes that "a vast majority of Peruvians, convinced that Vargas Llosa represented the white elite and that his program would place an unfair burden of the economic adjustment (demanded by first world lenders) onto the poor, voted against Vargas Llosa." Rudolph, *Peru: The Evolution of a Crisis* (Westport, CT: Praeger Publishers, 1992), 144.

SEA played an instrumental role in mobilizing the voting power of the poor in El Agustino. This was part of an ongoing effort to encourage the residents of the barrio to be agents for change in their own lives.

67. For more information, see María Cruz Saco, "Drawing More Lines: Factor Analyzing and Clustering Poverty in Peru," in *Congress of Latin American Studies Association* (Latin American Studies Association, 1992); Paul Glewwe and Dennis de Tray, "The Poor in Latin America during Adjustment: A Case Study of Peru" (Washington, DC: World Bank, 1989); and Glewwe, "The Distribution of Welfare in Peru, 1985" (Washington, DC: World Bank, 1988).

68. Henry Dietz, *Urban Poverty, Political Participation, and the State: Lima 1970–1990* (Pittsburgh: University of Pittsburgh, 1998), 64–65. Also see John Crabtree, *Peru Under García: An Opportunity Lost* (Pittsburgh: University of Pittsburgh Press, 1992), 143; and Luis La Madrid, "El Momento Económico," *Perú Económico* 13 (03 March 1990): 11–13.

69. Manuel M. Marzal, *Los Caminos Religiosos de los Inmigrantes en La Gran Lima: El Caso de El Agustino*, trans. Tom Powers, S.J. (Lima: Fondo Editorial de la Pontificia Universidad Católica del Perú, 1988), 36.

70. Modesta Centano Salazar, interview and translation by author, 11 February 1998, tape recording, SEA, Lima. While El Niño did not directly touch Lima in 1998, the eventual runoff from the mountains did result in flooding to those areas directly adjacent to the River Rímac, which flows through the city. The neighborhoods influenced are some of the poorest in Lima.

71. Instituto de Estadística Informática, *Censos Nacionales* (Lima: Instituto de Estadística e Informática, 1993).

72. José María García, "Pobreza, población y vivienda en distritos de Lima metropolitana," in *Lima: Población, trabajo, y política*, eds. Henríquez Narda et al. (Lima: Pontificia Universidad Católica, 1985), 113–134, 127–128.

73. Isabel Rivera Gónzales, *Síntesis de la experiencia de acompañamiento en las comunidades cristianas por agentes pastorales* (Lima: Parroquia La Virgen de Nazaret, 1996), 8.

74. Elena Decheco Egúsquiza, *50 Años de lucha y esperanza de El Agustino* (Lima: Inedito, 1996), 19.

75. For example, Defensoría Municipal del Niño y el Adolescente (Municipal Defense of Children and Adolescents or DEMUNA), a municipal agency; MAMIS, an outreach of the nearest state hospital, Hipólito Unanue Hospital; as well as agencies in the parish and others operated by NGOs publicize and work against domestic violence.

Statistics gathered by the federal organization *Ministerio de la promoción de las mujeres y desarrollo humano* (Ministry of the Promotion of Women and Human Development or PROMUDEH) indicate that while domestic violence is prevalent throughout Peruvian society, it is the lower social classes that are least apt to report it. There exists a widespread fear among poor women to press charges due to the inevitable consequences: increased fear and stress at home, ostracization by neighbors and family members, and dependence upon the aggressor for income in order to survive.

The number of cases of child abuse has increased at an annual rate of 15 percent in the past four years according to children's right organizations. Regretfully, it is estimated that 60 percent of cases go unreported. (See Miriam Schenone, Minister for the Promotion of Women and Human Development, interview and translation by author, tape recording, PROMUDEH, 03 March 1998, Lima).

76. For additional information see Carmen Pimentel Sevilla, ed. *Violencia, Familia y Niñez en los Sectores Urbanos Pobres* (Lima: Ramón Pajuelo, 1995); Human Rights Watch, "Untold Horror: Violence against Women in Peru's Armed Conflict" (New York: Human Rights Watch/Americas, 1998); Kristin Herzog, *Finding Their Voice: Peruvian Women's Testimony of War* (Valley Forge, PA: Trinity Press International, 1993); Nelson Figueroa Anaya and Asunta Montoya Rojas, *De Voces Sueños y Osadías: Mujeres Ejemplares del Perú* (Lima: Centro de Producción y Documentación Radiofónica, 1995), 63–66; Carmen Pimentel Sevilla, ed. *La Familia y Sus Problemas en los Sectores Urbanos Pobres* (Lima: Centro Comunitario de Salud Mental, 1996); Carmen Lora, Cecilia Barnachea, and Fryné Santisteban, *Mujer: Víctima de opresión, portadora de liberación* (Lima: Instituto Bartolomé de Las Casas, 1987); and Diana Miloslavich Tupac, *María Elena Moyano: En Busca de una Esperanza* (Lima: Centro de la Mujer Peruano Flora Tristan, 1993).

77. José Ignacio Mantecón, S.J., interview and translation by author, 27 February 1998, tape recording, La Virgen de Nazaret, Lima.

78. Marzal, *Caminos Religiosos de Los Inmigrantes en La Gran Lima*, 44–52.

79. Ofelia Montes López, interview and translation by author, 26 March 1998, tape recording, SEA, Lima.

80. The communal banks are instrumental in the promotion of small businesses.

81. Irene Silverblatt, "Moon, Sun, Witches," in *The Peru Reader: History, Culture, Politics*, eds. Orin Starn, Carlos Iván Degregori, and Robin Kirk (Durham, NC: Duke University Press, 1995), 35–48.

82. For instance, Micaela Bastidas, the wife of the famous nineteenth-century freedom fighter Tupac Amarú, fought with her husband and was executed by the

Spanish. See Carol Andreas, *When Women Rebel: The Rise of Popular Feminism in Peru* (Brooklyn: Lawrence Hill Books, 1985), 6. For additional information on Sra. Bastidas, see Herzog, *Finding Their Voice*, 21–24.

83. María Emma Mannarelli, 01 April 1998.

84. For example, see Norma Fuller, *Dilemas de la Feminidad: Mujeres de Clase Media en el Perú* (Lima: Pontificia Universidad Católica del Perú, 1993); and Carolina Carlessi, *Feminismo: Una Cuestión de Poder* (Lima: Movimiento Manuela Ramos, 1995).

85. Ofelia Montes López, 26 March 1998.

86. Andreas, *When Women Rebel*, 15.

87. Rosa Canto Castro, 18 February 1998.

88. For a thorough analysis of *machismo*, see Elsa Tamez, ed., *Against Machismo: Rubem Alves, Leonardo Boff, Gustavo Gutiérrez, José Miguez Bonino, Juan Luis Segundo and Others Talk about the Struggle of Women* (Oak Park, IL: Meyer-Stone Books, 1987); and Ray Gonzalez, ed. *Muy MacHo: Latino Men Confront Their Manhood* (Garden City, NY: Anchor Books/Doubleday, 1996).

89. Gutiérrez writes: "One thing that makes it very difficult to grasp (the) true character (of the unacceptable and inhuman character of women's lives) is it hiddenness, for it has become something habitual, part of everyday life and cultural tradition. So true is this that when we point it out we sound a bit like foreigners bent on causing trouble." Gutiérrez, "Expanding the View," in *Expanding the View: Gustavo Gutiérrez and the Future of Liberation Theology*, eds. Marc H. Ellis and Otto Maduro (Maryknoll, NY: Orbis Books, 1990), 6.

90. Lora, Barnachea, and Santisteban, *Mujer: Víctima de opresión*, 21.

91. María Emma Mannarelli, 01 April 1988.

92. *Manuela Ramos* is the Spanish equivalent of Jane Doe. It also carries the denotation of "everywoman."

93. Rosa Dominga Trapasso, interview by author, 30 January 1998, tape recording, Centro de Creatividad y Cambio (Center of Creativity and Change), Lima.

As early as 1971, Gutiérrez wrote of the inherent problems in governmental development programs.

> The term *development* has synthesized the aspiration of poor peoples during the last few decades. Recently, however, it has become the object of severe criticism due both to the deficiencies of the development policies proposed to the poor countries to lead them out of their underdevelopment and also to lack of concrete achievements of the interested governments. This is the reason why *developmentalism* (*desarrollismo*), a term derived from *development* (*desarrollo*), is now used in a pejorative sense, especially in Latin America. (Gutiérrez, *Theology of Liberation*, 16)

Regrettably, the situation of which Gutiérrez speaks has not changed a great deal in the intervening years. The negative context of the word *desarrollo* carries forth. This creates prejudicial sentiments regarding *El Ministerio de Promoción de la Mujer y del Desarrollo Humano.*

94. Benedicta Serrano Agüero, interview and translation by author, 20 February 1998, tape recording, SEA, Lima.

Chapter 3

1. Gloria Bravo Palomeque, interview and translation by author, 03 March 1998, tape recording, SEA, Lima.

2. Ibid.

3. Ofelia Montes López, 02 February 1998.

4. Irene Cáceres Sánchez, interview and translation by author, 02 March 1998, tape recording, SEA, Lima.

5. María Clara Bingemer, "Women in the Future of the Theology of Liberation," *SEDOS Bulletin* 22 (Fall 1990): 25–30.

6. Edelmira Aclari Castellares, interview and translation by author,11 February 1998, tape recording, SEA, Lima.

7. See Romic Nauta, "Latin American Women's Theology," *Exchange* 48 (1987): 8f.

8. María José F. Rosada Nunes (sic), "Women's Voices in Latin American Theology," *Concilium* 1 (1996): 5.

9. For example, see Lora, Barnachea, and Santisteban, *Mujer: Víctima de opresión, portadora de liberación;* Carmen Lora, *Creciendo en Dignidad: Movimiento de Comedores Autogestionarios* (Lima: CEP [Instituto Bartolomé de Las Casas]—Rímac, 1996); Consuelo del Prado and Amparo Huamán, "La mujer en la comunidad eclesial," *Páginas* 117 (September 1992): 102–110; and del Prado, "I Sense God in Another Way," in *Through Her Eyes: Women's Theology from Latin America*, ed. Elsa Tamez (Maryknoll, NY: Orbis Books, 1989). As Lucho Mejica, coordinator of the *Programa de Estudios Sociales* (Social Studies Program) at the *Instituto Bartolomé de Las Casas,* stated,

> The religious women in Peru are so busy that they have little or no time to reflect. This would be a wonderful source of theology from a woman's perspective if they were given the opportunity. The women in Peru who are trained theologically are either involved in other types of work (such as Carmen Lora and her psychological-pedagogical research) or are so intensely involved with their work with the poor that they have no time to write. I am thinking of Sisters Consuelo del Prado and Brigida Weiler. It should also be noted that Consuelo and Brigida are not from Peru. (Lucho Mejica, interview and

translation by author, 08 April 1998, tape recording, Instituto Bartolomé de Las Casas, Lima)

10. For example, the following books, hardly an exhaustive list, deal with one or more of these topics in a theological context: Nelson Figueroa Anaya and Asunta Montoya Rojas, *De Voces Sueños y Osadías;* Andreas, *When Women Rebel*; María Pilar Aquino, *Nuestro clamor por la vida;* Mary Field Belenky, Blythe McVicker, Nancy Rule Goldberger, and Jill Mattuck Tarule, *Women's Ways of Knowing: The Development of Self, Voice, and Mind*, 10th anniversary ed. (New York: Basic, 1997); Emilie Bergmann et al., *Women, Culture, and Politics in Latin America, Seminar on Feminism and Culture in Latin America* (Berkeley: University of California Press, 1990); Cecilia Blondet, *Las mujeres y el poder: Una historia de Villa El Salvador* (Lima: Instituto de Estudios Peruanos, 1991); Patricia Córdova Cayo, *Liderazgo Femenino en Lima: Estrategias de supervivencia* (Lima: Fundación Freidrich Ebert, 1996); Rebecca Chopp, *The Power to Speak: Feminism, Language, God* (New York: Crossroad, 1989); Patricia Córdova Cayo, ed. *Mujer Liderazgo: Entre la familia y la política* (Lima: Yunta, 1992); Virginia Fabella and Mercy Amba Oduyoye, eds. *With Passion and Compassion: Third World Women Doing Theology* (Maryknoll, NY: Orbix Books, 1996); Fabella and Sergio Torres, eds. *Doing Theology in a Divided World* (Maryknoll, NY: Orbis Books, 1985); Nancy Goldberger, Jill Tarule, Blythe Clinchy, and Mary Belenky, eds. *Knowledge, Difference, and Power: Essays Inspired by Women's Way of Knowing* (1996: Basic, 1996); Renny Golden, *The Hour of the Poor, The Hour of Women: Salvadoran Women Speak* (New York: Crossroads Publishing Company, 1991); Herzog, *Finding Their Voice*; Margaret Hooks, *Guatemalan Women Speak* (Washington, DC: EPICA, 1993); Elizabeth Jelin, ed. *Women and Social Change in Latin America* (London: Zed Books, 1990); Ofelia Ortega, ed. *Women's Visions: Theological Reflection, Celebration, and Action* (Geneva: WCC Publications, 1995); Elizabeth Say, *Evidence on Her Own Behalf: Women's Narrative as Theological Voice* (Savage, MD: Rowman & Littlefield, 1990); Elisabeth Schüssler Fiorenza, ed. *The Power of Naming: A Concilium Reader in Feminist Liberation Theology* (Maryknoll, NY: Orbis Books, 1996); Anne Thurston, *Because of Her Testimony: The Word in Female Experience* (New York: Crossroad Publishing Company, 1995); Elsa Tamez, ed. *Through Her Eyes: Women's Theology from Latin America* (Maryknoll, NY: Orbis Books, 1989); Elsa Tamez, ed. *Las Mujeres Toman la Palabra* (San José, Costa Rica: Editorial Departamento Ecunémico de Investigaciones, 1989); David Tracy, *On Naming the Present: Reflections on God, Hermeneutics, and Church* (Maryknoll, NY: Orbis Books, 1994); Maritza Villavicencio, *Del Silencio a la Palabra* (Lima: Centro de la Mujer Peruana Flora Tristan, 1992); and Meredith Tax, et al., *El Poder de la Palabra: Cultura, Censura y Voz* (Lima: Ediciones Flora Tristan, 1996).

11. This is a term used by feminist theologian Elisabeth Schüssler Fiorenza. See Fiorenza, ed. *Power of Naming*, 161.

12. José Ignacio Mantecón, S.J., 27 February 1998.

13. Rosa Canto Castro, 18 February 1998.

14. Golden, *Hour of the Poor*, 17.

15. I avoid the use of the modifier *feminist* in relation to the women in El Agustino for various reasons. First of all, it comes laden with European and North American significance—meanings that may not be appropriate for the context of El Agustino. Secondly, in over 120 hours of taped interviews (and countless more hours of unrecorded conversations), the term was utilized only by the secular feminists and professors at the PUC.

16. Gutiérrez, 25 February 1998. He continued on to say that "I was one of the writers for the documents for Puebla. Originally, the expression *doblemente oprimida, doblemente marginalizada* was in the text of the document but the conservative forces attempted to have it removed all together. A compromise was made and it appeared in a footnote." For the full official text and commentaries of the Puebla Conference, see John Eagleson and Philip Scharpter, eds. *Puebla and Beyond: Documentation and Commentary* (Maryknoll, NY: Orbis Books, 1979).

17. Celia Sánchez Rojas, interview and translation by author, 12 February 1998, tape recording, SEA, Lima.

18. Ivone Gebara, "Women Doing Theology in Latin America," in *With Passion and Compassion*, 126.

19. Zenaida Zúñiga Medina, interview and translation by author, 05 February 1998, tape recording, SEA, Lima.

20. Lucy Mejia Calderón, interview and translation by author, 10 February 1998, tape recording, *Comedor Independiente,* Lima.

21. Elvira Torres Anas, interview and translation by author, 07 February 1998, tape recording, SEA, Lima.

22. John Paul II, *The Church: Mystery, Sacrament, Community*, vol. 4 (Boston: Pauline Books and Media, 1998), 229.

23. John Paul II, *Ut Unum Sint* [http://listserv.american.edu/catholic/church/papal/jp.ii/jp2utunu.html] (American University, 1995, accessed 01 September, 1999), 94.

24. Ofelia Montes López, 03 March 1998.

25. Sally M. Vance-Trembath, "John Paul II's *Ut unum sint* and Conversation with Women," *Theological Studies* 60 1 (March 1999): 107–108.

26. Irene Cáceres Sánchez, 03 February 1998.

27. Carmen Férnandez Cano, interview and translation by author, 10 February 1998, tape recording, SEA, Lima.

28. Modesta Centano Salazar, 11 February 1998.

29. Elvira Torres Anas, 07 February 1998.

30. Martha Vera Belleza, interview and translation by author, 11 February 1998, tape recording, *La Panadería de La Virgen de Nazaret*, Lima.

31. Relinda Sosa Perez, interview and translation by author, 18 February 1999, tape recording, SEA, Lima.

32. Benedicta Serrano Agüero, 20 February 1998.

33. Quoted by David Tracy in Hans Küng and David Tracy, eds. *Paradigm Change in Theology: A Symposium for the Future* (New York: Crossroad Publishing Company, 1991), 35.

34. María Ramos Vega, interview and translation by author, 09 February 1998, tape recording, SEA, Lima.

35. Ofelia Montes López, 26 March 1998.

36. Gloria Bravo Palomeque, 28 March 1998.

37. Rosa Pacheco, 06 March 1998.

38. Edelmira Aclari Castellares, 11 February 1998.

39. Relinda Sosa Perez, 18 February 1998.

40. Esther Arteago Serrano, interview and translation by author, 23 February 1998, tape recording, SEA, Lima.

41. María Ramos Vega, 09 February 1998.

42. Benedicta Serrano Agüero, 18 February 1998.

43. Ibid.

44. Rosa Canto Castro, 18 February 1998.

45. Carmen Fernández Cano, 10 February 1998.

46. Frei Bretto, "God Burst Forth in the Experience of Life," in *The Idols of Death and the God of Life: A Theology,* eds. Pablo Richard et al. (Maryknoll, NY: Orbis Books, 1983), 163.

47. Rosa Pacheco, 06 March 1998.

48. Paulina Flores de Osorio, 26 February 1998.

50. Elvira Torres Anas, 07 February 1998.

51. Soraya Ronquillo Peña, interview and translation by author, 26 February 1998, tape recording, SEA, Lima.

52. Comisión Episcopal de Acción Social, *Between Honesty and Hope: Documents From and About the Church in Latin America* (Maryknoll, NY: Maryknoll Publications, 1970), 153.

53. Elvira Torres Anas, 07 February 1998.

54. María Ramos Vega, 09 February 1998.

55. Esther Arteago Serrano, 23 February 1998.

56. Brigida Weiler, interview and translation by author, 27 March 1998, Breña, Lima.

57. This will obviously not be in the near future. The Commission on Global Governance issued a report in 1995, which stated that

> the number of absolute poor, the truly destitute, was estimated by the World Bank at 1.3 billion in 1993, and is probably still growing. One fifth of the world lives in countries, mainly in Africa and Latin America, where living standards actually fell during the 1980s. Several indicators of aggregate poverty—1.5 billion lack access to safe water and 2 billion lack safe sanitation; more than 1 billion are illiterate, including half of the rural women—are no less chilling than a quarter century ago." (Commission on Global Governance, *Our Global Neighborhood* [Oxford: Oxford University Press, 1995], 139)

58. An excellent study of this process in the North American context may be found in Belenky, McVicker, Goldberger, and Mattuck Tarule, *Women's Ways of Knowing.*

59. Teresa Valdes Echenique and Enrique Gomariz Moraga, eds. *Mujeres Latinoamericanas en Cifras,* 21.

60. United Nations Development Programme, "Domestic Violence in Peru" (New York: United Nations, 1999), 2.

61. Sofia Macher, National Coordinator of Human Rights, interview and translation by author, 16 April 1998, tape recording, *Oficina de Derechos Humanos*, Lima.

62. Ibid.

63. Valdes Echenique and Gomariz Moraga, eds. *Mujeres Latinoamericanas en Cifras*, 55.

64. Sofia Macher, 16 April 1998.

65. Relinda Sosa Perez, 18 February 1998.

66. Celia Sánchez Rojas, 12 February 1998.

67. Modesta Centano Salazar, 11 February 1998.

68. Gloria Bravo Palomeque, 03 February 1998.

69. Benedicta Serrano Agüero, 20 February 1998.

70. María Ramos Vega, 09 February 1998.

Chapter 4

1. King, *Feminist Theology from the Third World*, 4.

2. Kathryn Tanner, *Theories of Culture: A New Agenda for Theology* (Minneapolis: Fortress Press, 1997), 63–64.

3. Ibid., 64.

4. Austin Ivereigh, "Jesuit Mission in Gangland," *Tablet* (25 March 2000): 408.

5. Tanner, *Theories of Culture,* 69.

6. Ibid., 70.

7. The 1994 Oregon "Death with Dignity" legislation brought this topic fully into the legal arena.

8. Søren Kierkegaard, *Journals,* trans. Alexander Dru (London: Oxford University Press, 1938), 343.

9. M. Shawn Copeland, "Wading through Many Sorrows: Toward a Theology of Suffering in Womanist Perspective," in *A Troubling in My Soul: Womanist Perspectives on Evil and Suffering*, ed. Emilie M. Townes (Maryknoll, NY: Orbis Books, 1993), 109.

10. See also Matt. 26:11 and Mark 14:7.

11. Kristine M. Rankka presents a detailed and erudite examination of this topic in her book on suffering. See Rankka, *Women and the Value of Suffering: An Aw(e)ful Rowing toward God* (Collegeville, MN: Liturgical Press, 1998).

12. Copeland, "Wading Through Many Sorrows," 109.

13. Ofelia Montes López, 02 February 1998.

14. Zenaida Medina Zúñiga, 05 February 1998.

15. Rosa Canto Castro, 18 February 1998.

16. Eleazar S. Fernandez, *Toward a Theology of Struggle* (Maryknoll, NY: Orbis Books, 1994), 19.

17. The word *theodicy* comes from the Greek *theos* (God) and *dike* (justice). Theodicies are developed in an attempt to justify belief in God's goodness when faced with suffering and evil in the world. Inherent in this discussion is the questioning of how a God who is all-powerful would allow evil to exist. Theologians stress human free will as the instigator of evil (not that of a "creation" of a loving God), the ultimate ineffability of God, and the fact that the reign of God is not complete but yet to come. For additional discussion of theodicies, see Johannes Baptist Metz, *A Passion for God: The Mystical-Political Dimension of Christianity*, ed. and trans. Ashley J. Matthew (New York: Paulist Press, 1998); Brian Hebblewaite, *Evil, Suffering, and Religion* (New York: Hawthorn Books, 1976); Rankka, *Women and the Value of Suffering*; and David Birnbaum, *God and Evil: A Unified Theodicy/Theology/Philosophy* (Hoboken, NJ: Ktav Publishing House, 1989).

18. Modesta Centano Salazar, 11 February 1998.

19. Soraya Ronquillo Peña, 26 February 1998.

20. Martha Vera Belleza, 02 February 1998.

21. See in particular Gutiérrez, *On Job: God-Talk and the Suffering of the Innocent*, trans. Matthew J. O'Connell (Maryknoll, NY: Orbis Books, 1986).

22. Celia Sánchez Rojas, 12 February 1998.

23. There have also been women who no longer work for SEA for other reasons, such as a newborn child or the necessity of a better paying job.

24. Gloria Bravo Palomeque, 03 February 1998.

25. Irene Cáceres Sánchez, 03 February 1998.

26. Elvira Torres Anas, 07 February 1998.

27. Zenaida Zúñiga Medina, 05 February 1998.

28. Martha Vera Belleza, 02 February 1998.

29. Zenaida Zúñiga Medina, 05 February 1998.

30. Benedicta Serrano Agüero, 20 February 1998.

31. Ibid.

32. Relinda Sosa Perez, 18 February 1998.

33. Gutiérrez's question was, "How do we speak of God to the people of Ayacucho?"

34. Ofelia Montes López, 26 March 1998.

35. José Comblin, *Retrieving the Human: A Christian Anthropology* (*Theology and Liberation Series*), trans. Robert R. Barr (Maryknoll, NY: Orbis Books: 1990), 1.

36. The word *barriada* translates into English as "slum." The use of this word, in lieu of the commonly accepted *pueblo joven*, is an indication of the nonacceptance of the millions of poor in Lima on the part of a wealthy minority.

37. Modesta Centano Salazar, 11 February 1998.

38. Lucy Mejia Calderón, 10 February 1998.

39. Elvira Torres Anas, 07 February 1998.

40. Ofelia Montes López, 26 March 1998.

41. Relinda Sosa Perez, 18 February 1998.

42. Jaime O'Leary, S.J., interview by author, 02 April 1998, tape recording, *Fe y Alegría*, Lima.

43. Irene Cáceres Sánchez, 03 February 1998.

44. Martha Vera Belleza, 02 February 1998.

45. Paulo Freire, *Pedagogy of the Oppressed* (New York: Continuum Publishing Company, 1994), 134.

46. Freire, *The Politics of Education* (Westport, CT: Bergin and Garvey, 1985), xii.

47. Ofelia Montes López, 26 March 1998.

48. Rosa Castillo Reyes, interview and translation by author, 24 February 1998, tape recording, SEA, Lima.

49. Paulina Flores de Osorio, 26 February 1998.

50. María Ramos Vega, 09 February 1998.

51. Ofelia Montes López, 02 February 1998.

52. Soraya Ronquillo Peña, 26 February 1998.

53. Juan Luis Segundo, an Uruguayan Jesuit liberation theologian wrote of a "suspicion that theology, like other all-pervasive cultural features, can and perhaps should be considered an instrument of oppression and, hence, as a non-Christian theology." Juan Luis Segundo, "The Shift Within Latin American Theology," *Journal of Theology for Southern Africa* 52 (1985): 22. The women of El Agustino have learned from experience that a healthy suspicion is necessary for survival.

54. Mary Magdalene appears in all four Gospels. In addition to Matthew, she is found in Mark 15–16, Luke 24, and John 19–20.

55. Modesta Centano Salazar, group meeting, 14 March 1998.

56. Celia Sánchez Rojas, group meeting, 14 March 1998.

57. Ofelia Montes López, group meeting, 14 March 1998.

58. The women occasionally use a book on biblical interpretation. The outside facilitators who are invited to participate normally do just that—facilitate—and they do not turn the reflection group into a lecture.

59. Relinda Sosa Perez, group meeting, 14 March 1998.

60. Elvira Torres Anas, 07 February 1998.

61. Gloria Bravo Palomeque, 03 February 1998.

62. Rosa Castillo Reyes, 24 February 1998.

63. An examination of this in the North American context may be found in Craig L. Nessan, *Orthopraxis or Heresy: The North American Theological Response to Latin American Liberation Theology*, ed. Susan Thistlewaite (Atlanta: Scholars Press, 1989).

64. Hennelly, *Liberation Theology*, 95.

65. Zenaida Zúñiga Medina, 05 February 1998.

66. Karl Rahner, *Foundations of Christian Faith: An Introduction to the Idea of Christianity*, trans. William V. Dych (New York: Seabury Press, 1978), 138–175.

67. Most of the information outlined in this section came from interviews with various people in the barrio.

68. MIADES were also initiated in the barrios of Villa El Salvador (1983), and Comas and Arte Vitarte (1989).

69. Francisco Chamberlain, S.J., 16 February 1998.

70. The facts and stories in this section are derived from my interviews with Ofelia Montes López and Soraya Ronquillo Peña, both administrators for SEA.

71. Ofelia Montes López, 26 March 1998.

72. Soraya Ronquillo Peña, 26 February 1998.

73. Ibid.

74. Ethicist Fr. Daniel Hartnett, S.J. developed the concept of ACAS in the early years of his work with SEA.

75. Humberto Ortiz R., *Las Organizaciones Económicas Populares: Semillas pequeñas para grandes cambios* (Lima: Servicios Educativos El Agustino, 1993), 15.

76. Margarita Córdova Herrera, interview and translation by author, 01 April 1998, tape recording, SEA, Lima.

77. Sofía Macher, 16 April 1998 and Ofelia Montes López, 25 March 1998.

78. Rosa Pacheco, 06 March 1998.

79. Ofelia Montes López, 26 March 1998.

80. Benedicta Serrano Agüero, 20 February 1998.

81. Ofelia Montes López, 26 March 1998.

82. Catholic Caritas organizations operate in many countries providing financial and hard goods assistance to various third world countries. Interestingly, Denmark has an estimated Catholic population of only 7 percent yet the Caritas there has supported programs of SEA since 1983.

83. María Ramos Vega, 09 February 1998.

84. Elena Decheco, interview and translation by author, 23 March 1998, tape recording, SEA, Lima.

85. Sofía Macher, 16 April 1998.

86. Blondet and Carmen Montero, *La Situación de la Mujer en el Perú: 1980–1984* (Lima: IEP Ediciones, 1995), 87.

87. Twenty-six percent of the cases reported in Lima in 1993 involved drugs and/or alcohol. Ibid., 87.

88. Carmen Lora, interview and translation by author, 05 March 1998, tape recording, Instituto Bartolomé de Las Casas, Lima.

89. Rosa Castillo Reyes, 24 February 1998.

90. "No one can serve two masters. Either he will hate the one and love the other, or he will be devoted to the one and despise the other. You cannot serve both God and money" (Matt 6:24).

91. Ofelia Montes López, 02 February 1998.

92. *Centesimus Annus*, no. 33. The complete English translation may be found in David J. O'Brien and Thomas A. Shannon, eds. *Catholic Social Thought: The Documentary Heritage* (Maryknoll, NY: Orbis Books, 1992).

93. Ofelia Montes López, 02 February 1998.

94. Lucy Mejia Calderón, 10 February 1998.

95. Modesta Centano Salazar, 11 February 1998.

96. Irene Cáceres Sánchez, 03 February 1998.

97. Leonardo Boff, OFM, *Faith on the Edge: Religion and Marginalized Existence* (San Francisco: Harper, 1989), 158.

98. Esther Arteago Serrano, 23 February 1998.

Chapter 5

1. Schreiter, *New Catholicity*, 98.

2. Soraya Ronquillo Peña, 26 February 1998.

3. Benedicta Serrano Agüero, 20 February 1998.

4. Miriam Schenone, interview and translation by author, 03 March 1998, tape recording, *Ministerio de Promoción de la Mujer y del Desarrollo Humano*, Lima.

5. Teresa Valdes Echenique and Enrique Gomariz Moraga, eds. *Mujeres Latinoamericanas en Cifras,* 37.

6. Liliana Ramirez, interview and translation by author, 17 April 1998, tape recording, Movimiento Manuela Ramos, Lima.

7. Soraya Ronquillo Peña, 26 February 1998.

8. Relinda Sosa Perez, 18 February 1998.

9. Juan Luis Cipriani Thorne, *Homilía pronunciada por su Excelencia, el Arzobispo de Lima y Primado del Perú* (Lima: Arquidiócesis de Lima, 1999).

10. Ofelia Montes López, 07 February 2000.

11. Gloria Apaza Cruz, interview and translation by author, 28 March 1998, tape recording, SEA, Lima.

12. Gutiérrez, 25 February 1998.

13. Ian Linden, *Liberation Theology Coming of Age?* (London: CIIR, 1997), 50.

14. Gutiérrez, "The Task and Content of Liberation Theology," in *The Cambridge Companion to Liberation Theology,* ed. Christopher Rowland (Cambridge: Cambridge University Press, 1999), 19.

15. See, for example, King, *Feminist Theology from the Third World;* Rosemary Radford Ruether, *Liberation Theology: Human Hope Confronts Christian History and American Power* (New York: Paulist Press, 1972); and Ada María Isasi-Díaz and Yolando Tarango, *Hispanic Women: Prophetic Voice in the Church* (Minneapolis: Fortress Press, 1992).

16. See James H. Cone, *A Black Theology of Liberation*, 20th Anniversary ed. (Maryknoll, NY: Orbis Books, 1990); and Ada María Isasi-Díaz and Fernando F. Segovia, eds. *Hispanic/Latino Theology: Challenge and Promise* (Minneapolis: Fortress Press, 1996).

17. See Marzal, *Los Caminos Religiosos de los Inmigrantes en La Gran Lima.*

18. See Boff, *Cry of the Earth, Cry of the Poor* (Maryknoll, NY: Orbis Books, 1997).

19. See Naim Stifan Ateek, *Justice and Only Justice: Toward a Palestinian Theology of Liberation* (Maryknoll, NY: Orbis Books, 1990); and Metz, *Passion for God.*

20. See Hyun K. Chung, *Struggle to Be the Sun Again: Introducing Asian Women's Theology* (Maryknoll, NY: Orbis Books, 1991).

21. See Marc H. Ellis, *Toward a Jewish Theology of Liberation* (Maryknoll, NY: Orbis Books, 1987); and Farid Esack, *Qur'an, Liberation and Pluralism: An Islamic Perspective of Interreligious Solidarity Against Oppression* (Oxford: Oneworld Publications, 1997).

22. Zenaida Zúñiga Medina, 05 February 1998.

23. Synod of Bishops, *Justice in the World* [http://www.osjpm.org/cst/jw.htm] (1971, accessed 14 November 1999), 6.

24. Synod of Bishops, *Justice in the World*, 36.

25. Ibid., 34.

26. Boff, *Church, Charism and Power* (New York: Crossroad Publishing Company, 1990), 12.

27. Zenaida Zúñiga Medina, 05 February 1998.

Vocational training helps women prepare for jobs outside the home.

Glossary of Spanish Words and Terms

ACAS (*acompañamiento, capacitación, asesoría, sistematización*)—accompaniment, encouragement, assessing, systemizing

Acción Popular—Popular Action political party

Actor popular—community organizer

Altiplano—high-altitude plateau

Ama de casa—housewife

Ambulante—street merchant

Aprista (*Alianza Popular Revolucionaria Americana* or **APRA**)—Popular Revolutionary American Alliance

Asociación de Industrias en Desarrollo de El Agustino—El Agustino Association of Industries in Development

Autogolpe—self-coup

Bancos comunales—communal banks

Barriada—slum

Barrio—neighborhood

Basura—garbage

Cambio 90—Change 90, political party of Alberto Fujimori

campesina (campesino)—peasant farmer

Casa Nuestra Señora de Fátima—Our Lady of Fatima House

Centro de Creatividad y Cambio—Center of Creativity and Change

Centro de Estudios y Publicaciones—Center of Studies and Publications or CEP

Centro de la Mujer Peruana Flora Tristan—Flora Tristan Peruvian Woman's Center

Centro Nacional de Organizaciones Sociales de Base—National Center of Base Social Organizations

Centros de Educación Ocupacional—Occupational Education Centers

Circuito metodológico—methodological circuit

Claustro—cloister

Club de Madres—Mothers' Club

Comedores populares—communal dining rooms

Comisión de Saneamiento Físico-Legal (COSFIL)—Sanitation Commission

Comisión episcopal de acción social (CEAS)—Bishops Commission of Social Action

Comité de Damas—Women's Committee

Comité de Lucha—Committee of Struggle

Comité de Salud—Health Committee

Comité Unico Vecinal Feminino—Women's Neighborhood Committee

Compañera(o)—companion

Congreso de acción social (CAS)—Congress of Social Action

Congreso Nacional de las Mujeres—National Women's Congress

Consejo Episcopal Latinoamericano (CELAM)—Council of Latin American Bishops

Coordinadora Nacional de Derechos Humanos (CNDDHH)—National Coordinator of Human Rights

Criollo—African Peruvian

Cursillos—short courses

Delegación de Mujeres—Women's Delegation

Delegación de Mujeres de la Capital—Women's Capital Delegation

Departamento—province, state, or department

Directiva Central del Pueblo—Town Council

Directora—Director

Educación Popular—Popular Education

Encomienda—Grants of land made by Spanish Kings

Encuentro—meeting

Equipo de Proyectos Empresariales—Business Projects Team

Equipo Mujer—Women's Team

Escollos—Pitfalls

Espacio social—social space

Fe y Alegría—Movimiento de Educación Popular Integral—Faith and Joy—Popular Education Movement

Federación de Mercados—Public Market Federation

Federación Departamental de Pueblos Jóvenes y Urbanizaciones Populares (FEDEPJUP)—Federation of Young Towns and Popular Urbanizations

Federación Popular de Mujeres—Women's Federation

Feminismo—feminism

Funeraria, La—funeral home

Indigena—indigenous person

Instituto Bartolomé de Las Casas—Bartolomé de Las Casas Institute (leading Latin American Liberation Theology Research Center)

Izquierda Unida—United Left Popular Party

Jornada—workday

Ley de reforma educativa, La—Educational Reform Law, The

Liberador, El—Liberator, The

Llamada de Dios—call of God

Loca(o)—crazy

Lógica de cosumo—economics of survival

Lógica empresarial—economics of accumulation

Lucha—struggle

Mercado Mayorista—Wholesale Market

Mestiza(o)—person of mixed race

Mezcla—mixture

Micro-Areas de Desarrollo (MIADES)—Small Areas of Development

Micro-empresarios—businesspeople operating small ventures

Ministerio de Promoción de la Mujer y del Desarrollo Humano, El (PROMUDEH)—Ministry of Promotion of Women and Human Development, The

Misión de Lima, La—Mission of Lima, The

Monjas—Religious women or nuns

Movimiento de los niños—Children's Movement

Movimiento de Trabajadores Cristianos—Christian Workers Movement

Movimiento Manuela Ramos—Manuela Ramos ("everywoman") Movement

Movimiento Revolucionario Tupac Amarú (MRTA)—Revolutionary Movement Tupac Amarú

Oficina nacional de información social (ONIS)—National Office of Social Information

Oficina nacional de la educación católica (ONDEC)—National Office of Catholic Education

Organizaciones Economicas Populares—public business organizations

Organizaciones Vecinales—neighborhood organizations

Pachamama—Mother Earth

Pais de las maravillas, un—A country of marvels

Palabras magicas, las—magic words, the

Panadería—bakery

Partera—midwife

Partido democristianos (PDC)—Christian Democratic Party

Partido Unión Popular (PUP)—Popular Union Party

Plan de desarrollo Distrital—District Development Plan

Pontificia Universidad Católica del Perú (PUC)—Pontifical Catholic University of Peru

Primera Semana Social—First Social Week

Provocador—instigator or fomenter

Proyecto de los Bancos Comuniales—Communal Banks Project

Pueblo joven (*pueblos jóvenes*)—young town(s)

Senderista—member of Sendero Luminoso

Sendero Luminoso—Shining Path

Señor de los Milagros, El—Lord of Miracles, The

Servicios Educativos El Agustino (SEA)—Educational Services El Agustino

Vaso de Leche—Glass of Milk (Children's Food Program)

Virgen de Nazaret, La—Virgin of Nazareth, The

Zonas de Tratamiento Especial (ZTE)—Zones of Special Treatment

Bibliography

Americas Watch. *Peru under Fire: Human Rights since the Return to Democracy*. New Haven, CT: Yale University Press, 1992.

Andreas, Carol. *When Women Rebel: The Rise of Popular Feminism in Peru*. Brooklyn: Lawrence Hill Books, 1985.

Aquino, María Pilar. *Nuestro clamor por la vida: Teología latino-americana desde la perspectiva de la mujer*. San José, Costa Rica: Editorial DEI, 1992.

Arrupe, Pedro, S.J. "Marxist Analysis by Christians." In *Liberation Theology: A Documentary History*, ed. Alfred T. Hennelly, 307–313. Maryknoll, NY: Orbis Books, 1980.

Ateek, Naim Stifan. *Justice and Only Justice: Towards a Palestinian Theology of Liberation*. Maryknoll, NY: Orbis Books, 1990.

Beik, Doris and Paul Beik. *Flora Tristan, Utopian Feminist: Her Travel Diaries and Personal Crusade*. Indianapolis: Indiana University Press, 1993.

Belenky, Mary Field, Blythe McVicker, Nancy Rule Goldberger, and Jill Mattuck Tarule. *Women's Ways of Knowing: The Development of Self, Voice, and Mind*, 10th anniversary ed. New York: Basic, 1997.

Bergmann, Emilie et al. *Women, Culture, and Politics in Latin America/Seminar on Feminism and Culture in Latin America*. Berkeley: University of California Press, 1990.

Bevans, Stephen B. *Models of Contextual Theology*, ed. Robert J. Schreiter. Maryknoll, NY: Orbis Books, 1998.

Bingemer, María Clara. "Women in the Future of the Theology of Liberation." *SEDOS Bulletin* 22 (Fall 1990): 25–30.

Birnbaum, David. *God and Evil: A Unified Theodicy/Theology/Philosophy*. Hoboken, NJ: Ktav Publishing House, 1989.

Blondet, Cecilia. *Las mujeres y el poder: Una historia de Villa El Salvador*. Lima: Instituto de Estudios Peruanos, 1991.

——— and Carmen Montero. *La Situación de la Mujer en el Perú: 1980–1984*. Lima: IEP Ediciones, 1995.

Boff, Leonardo. *Cry of the Earth, Cry of the Poor*. Maryknoll, NY: Orbis Books, 1997.

———. *Faith on the Edge: Religion and Marginalized Existence*. San Francisco: Harper, 1989.

———. *Church, Charism and Power*. New York: Crossroad Publishing Company, 1990.

Bretto, Frei. "God Burst Forth in the Experience of Life." In *The Idols of Death and the God of Life: A Theology*, eds. Pablo Richard et al. Maryknoll, NY: Orbis Books, 1983.

Burt, Jo Marie and Aldo Panfichi. *Peru: Caught in the Crossfire*. Jefferson City, MO: Peru Peace Movement/USA, 1992.

Carlessi, Carolina. *Feminismo: Una Cuestión de Poder*. Lima: Movimiento Manuela Ramos, 1995.

Castañeda, Jorge. *Utopia Unarmed: The Latin American Left after the Cold War*. New York: Vintage Books, 1991.

Chopp, Rebecca. *The Power to Speak: Feminism, Language, God*. New York: Crossroad, 1989.

Chung, Hyun K. *Struggle to Be the Sun Again: Introducing Asian Women's Theology*. Maryknoll, NY: Orbis Books, 1991.

Cipriani Thorne, Juan Luis. *Homilía pronunciada por su Excelencia, el Arzobispo de Lima y Primado del Perú*. Lima: Arquidiócesis de Lima, 1999.

Comblin, José. *Retrieving the Human: A Christian Anthropology*, trans. Robert R. Barr. Maryknoll, NY: Orbis Books, 1990.

Comisión Episcopal de Acción Social. *Between Honesty and Hope: Documents from and about the Church in Latin America*. Maryknoll, NY: Maryknoll Publications, 1970.

Commercial Data International. Country Review: Peru 1998/1999. Houston: Commercial, 1999.

Commission on Global Governance. *Our Global Neighborhood*. Oxford: Oxford University Press, 1995.

Cone, James H. *A Black Theology of Liberation*, 20th anniversary ed. Maryknoll, NY: Orbis Books, 1990.

Copeland, M. Shawn. "Wading through Many Sorrows: Toward a Theology of Suffering in Womanist Perspective." In *A Troubling in My Soul: Womanist Perspectives on Evil and Suffering*, ed. Emilie M. Townes. Maryknoll, NY: Orbis Books, 1993.

Córdova Cayo, Patricia. *Liderazgo Femenino en Lima: Estrategias de supervivencia*. Lima: Fundación Freidrich Ebert, 1996.

———, ed. *Mujer y Liderazgo: Entre la familia y política*. Lima: Yunta, 1992.

Crabtree, John. *Peru under García: An Opportunity Lost*. Pittsburgh: University of Pittsburgh Press, 1992.

Cruz Saco, María. "Drawing More Lines: Factor Analyzing and Clustering Poverty in Peru." In *Congress of Latin American Studies Association*: Latin American Studies Association, 1992.

Decheco Egúsquiza, Elena. *50 Años de lucha y esperanza de El Agustino*. Lima: Inedito, 1996.

Degregori, Carlos Iván. *Que difícil es Ser Dios: Ideología y Violencia Política en Sendero Luminoso*. Lima: Zorro de Abajo Ediciones, 1989.

del Prado, Consuelo. "I Sense God in Another Way." In *Through Her Eyes: Women's Theology from Latin America*, ed. Elsa Tamez, 140–149. Maryknoll, NY: Orbis Books, 1989.

——— and Amparo Huamán. "La mujer en la comunidad eclesial." *Páginas* 117 (September 1992): 102–110.

Dietz, Henry. *Urban Poverty, Political Participation, and the State: Lima 1970–1990*. Pittsburgh: University of Pittsburgh Press, 1998.

Dussel, Enrique D. "Theology of Liberation and Marxism." In *Mysterium Liberationis: Fundamental Concepts of Liberation Theology*, eds. Ignacio Ellacuría, S.J. and Jon Sobrino, S.J. Maryknoll, NY: Orbis Books, 1993.

Eagleson, John and Phillip Scharper, eds. *Puebla and Beyond: Documentation and Commentary*. Maryknoll, NY: Orbis Books, 1979.

Ellis, Marc H. *Toward a Jewish Theology of Liberation*. Maryknoll, NY: Orbis Books, 1987.

Esack, Farid. *Qu'ran, Liberation and Pluralism: An Islamic Perspective of Interreligious Solidarity Against Oppression*. Oxford: Oneworld Publications, 1997.

Fabella, Virginia and Mercy Amba Oduyoye, eds. *With Passion and Compassion: Third World Women Doing Theology*. Maryknoll, NY: Orbis Books, 1996.

——— and Sergio Torres, eds. *Doing Theology in a Divided World*. Maryknoll, NY: Orbis Books, 1985.

Fernandez, Eleazar S. *Toward a Theology of Struggle*. Maryknoll, NY: Orbis Books, 1994.

Figueroa Anaya, Nelson and Asunta Montoya Rojas. *De Voces Sueños y Osadías: Mujeres Ejemplares del Perú*. Lima: Centro de Producción y Documentación Radiofónica, 1995.

Foster, George. "Peasant Society and the Image of the Limited Good." *American Anthropologist* 67 (April 1965): 293–315.

Freire, Paulo. *The Politics of Education.* Westport, CT: Bergin and Garvey, 1985.

———. *Pedagogy of the Oppressed.* New York: Continuum Publishing, 1994.

Fuller, Norma. *Dilemas de la Feminidad: Mujeres de Clase Media en el Perú.* Lima: Pontificia Universidad Católica del Perú, 1993.

García, José María. "Pobreza, población y vivienda en distritos de Lima metropolitana." In *Lima: Población, trabajo, y política*, eds. Narda Henriquez et al., 113–134. Lima: Pontificia Universidad Católica, 1985.

Gebara, Ivone. "Women Doing Theology in Latin America." In *With Passion and Compassion: Third World Women Doing Theology*, eds. Virginia Fabella and Mercy Amba Oduyoye. Maryknoll, NY: Orbis Books, 1996.

Glewwe, Paul. *The Distribution of Welfare in Peru, 1985.* Washington, DC: World Bank, 1988.

——— and Dennis de Tray. *The Poor in Latin America During Adjustment: A Case Study of Peru.* Washington, DC: World Bank, 1989.

Goldberger, Nancy, Jill Tarule, Blythe Clinchy, and Mary Belenky, eds. *Knowledge, Difference, and Power: Essays Inspired by Women's Way of Knowing.* New York: Basic, 1996.

Golden, Renny. *The Hour of the Poor, The Hour of Women; Salvadoran Women Speak.* New York: Crossroad Publishing Company, 1991.

Gorriti Ellenbogen, Gustavo. *Sendero: Historia de la Guerra Milenaria en el Perú.* Lima: Editorial Apoyo, 1991.

Gutiérrez, Gustavo. *On Job: God-Talk and the Suffering of the Innocent.* Trans. Matthew J. O'Connell. Maryknoll, NY: Orbis Books, 1986.

———. "Expanding the View." In *Expanding the View: Gustavo Gutiérrez and the Future of Liberation Theology*, eds. Marc H. Ellis and Otto Maduro, 3–36. Maryknoll, NY: Orbis Books, 1990.

———. *A Theology of Liberation.* Trans. Sister Caridad Inda and John Eagleson, 15th anniversary ed. Maryknoll, NY: Orbis Books, 1994.

———. *Las Casas: In Search of the Poor of Jesus Christ.* Trans. Robert R. Barr. Maryknoll, NY: Orbis Books, 1995.

———. "The Task and Content of Liberation Theology." In *The Cambridge Companion to Liberation Theology*, ed. Christopher Rowland. Cambridge: Cambridge University Press, 1999.

Hall, Douglas John. *Thinking the Faith: Christian Theology in a North American Context.* Minneapolis: Fortress Press, 1991.

Hebblewaite, Brian. *Evil, Suffering, and Religion.* New York: Hawthorn Books, 1976.

Hélder Câmara, Dom. *Church and Colonialism*. Trans. William McSweeney. Denville, NJ: Dimension Books, 1969.

Hennelly, Alfred T., ed. *Liberation Theology: A Documentary History*. Maryknoll, NY: Orbis Books, 1990.

Herzog, Kristin. *Finding Their Voice: Peruvian Women's Testimony of War*. Valley Forge, PA: Trinity Press International, 1993.

Human Rights Watch. *Untold Horror: Violence against Women in Peru's Armed Conflict*. New York: Human Rights Watch/Americas, 1998.

Hutchison, Robert. *Their Kingdom Come: Inside the Secret World of Opus Dei*. New York: St. Martin's, 1999.

Illich, Ivan. "The Seamy Side of Charity." *America* (21 January 1967).

———. "The Seamy Side of Charity." In *Roman Catholic Church in Modern Latin America*, ed. Karl Michael Schmitt, 153–163. New York: Knopf, 1972.

Instituto de Estadística Informática. *Censos Nacionales*. Lima: Instituto de Estadística e Informática, 1993.

Isasi-Díaz, Ada María, and Fernando F. Segovia, eds. *Hispanic/Latino Theology: Challenge and Promise*. Minneapolis: Fortress Press, 1996.

——— and Yolanda Tarango, *Hispanic Women: Prophetic Voice in the Church*. Minneapolis: Fortress Press, 1992.

Isbell, Billie Jean. "Shinning Path and Peasant Responses in Rural Ayacucho." In *The Shining Path of Peru*, ed. David Scott Palmer. New York: St. Martin's, 1992.

Ivereigh, Austin. "Jesuit Mission in Gangland." *Tablet* (25 March 2000): 408.

Jelin, Elizabeth, ed. *Women and Social Change in Latin America*. London: Zed Books, 1990.

John Paul II. *The Church: Mystery, Sacrament, Community*, vol. 4. Boston: Pauline Books and Media, 1998.

Kierkegaard, Søren. *Journals*. Trans. Alexander Dru. London: Oxford University Press, 1938.

King, Ursula, ed. *Feminist Theology from the Third World: A Reader*. Maryknoll, NY: SPCK/Orbis Press, 1994.

Kirk, Robin. *Untold Terror: Violence against Women in Peru's Armed Conflict*. New York: Human Rights Watch, 1998.

Klaiber, Jeffrey. *The Catholic Church in Peru, 1821–1985: A Social History*. Washington, DC: Catholic University of America Press, 1992.

———. "The Church in Peru, Ecuador and Bolivia." In *The Church in Latin America: 1492–1992*, ed. Enrique Dussel. Maryknoll, NY: Orbis Books, 1992.

Küng, Hans and David Tracy, eds. *Paradigm Change in Theology: A Symposium for the Future*. New York: Crossroad Publishing Company, 1991.

La Madrid, Luis. "El Momento Económico." *Perú Económico* 13 (03 March 1990): 11–13.

Linden, Ian. *Liberation Theology Coming of Age?* London: CIIR, 1997.

Lora, Carmen. *Creciendo en Dignidad: Movimiento de Comedores Autogestionarios*. Lima: CEP (Instituto Bartolomé de Las Casas—Rímac), 1996.

———, Cecilia Barnachea, and Fryné Santisteban. *Mujer: Víctima de opresión, portadora de liberación*. Lima: Instituto Bartolomé de las Casas, 1987.

Madison, G. B. *Globalization: Challenges and Opportunities*. Hamilton, Ontario: McMaster University Institute on Globalization and the Human Condition, 1998.

Marzal, Manuel M. *Los Caminos Religiosos de Los Inmigrantes en La Gran Lima: El Caso de El Agustino*. Lima: Fondo Editorial de la Pontificia Universidad Católica del Perú, 1988.

Maza, Luis. "The Emergence and Development of *Sendero Luminoso* in Peru." *McNair Journal*, 1994.

Metz, Johann Baptist. "Theology in the Struggle for History and Society." In *Expanding the View: Gustavo Gutiérrez and the Future of Liberation Theology*, eds. Marc H. Ellis and Otto Maduro. Maryknoll, NY: Orbis Books, 1990.

———. *A Passion for God: The Mystical-Political Dimension of Christianity*. Ed. and trans. J. Matthew Ashley. New York: Paulist Press, 1998.

Miloslavic Tupac, Diana. *María Elena Moyano: En Busca de una Esperanza*. Lima: Centro de la Mujer Peruana Flora Tristan, 1993.

Nauta, Romic. "Latin American Women's Theology." *Exchange* 48 (1987): 8f.

Nessan, Craig L. *Orthopraxis or Heresy: The North American Theological Response to Latin American Liberation Theology*, ed. Susan Thistlewaite. Atlanta: Scholars Press, 1989.

Nickoloff, James B., ed. *Gustavo Gutiérrez: Essential Writings. The Making of Modern Theology*. Minneapolis: Fortress Press, 1996.

O'Brien, David J. and Thomas A. Shannon, eds. *Catholic Social Thought: The Documentary Heritage*. Maryknoll, NY: Orbis Books, 1992.

Oficina Nacional de Educación Católica. "Centros educacionales dirigidos por religiosos: estudio de su distribución por dioceses." Lima: Oficina Nacional de Educación Católica, 1971.

Ortega, Ofelia, ed. *Women's Visions: Theological Reflection, Celebration, and Action*. Geneva: WCC Publications, 1995.

Ortiz, R. Humberto. *Las Organizaciones Economicas Populares: Semillas pequeñas para grandes cambios.* Lima: Servicios Educativos El Agustino, 1993.

Palmer, David Scott. *The Shining Path of Peru.* New York: St. Martin's, 1992.

Pimentel Sevilla, Carmen, ed. *Violencia, Familia y Niñez en Los Sectores Urbanos Pobres.* Lima: Ramón Pajuelo, 1995.

———, ed. *La Familia y Sus Problemas en los Sectores Urbanos Pobres.* Lima: Centro Comunitario de Salud Mental, 1996.

Pinnock, Clark. *Tracking the Maze.* San Francisco: Harper, 1990.

Poole, Deborah and Gerardo Rénique. *Peru: Time of Fear.* London: Latin American Bureau, 1992.

Rahner, Karl. *Foundations of Christian Faith: An Introduction to the Idea of Christianity.* Trans. William V. Dych. New York: Seabury Press, 1978.

Rankka, Kristine M. *Women and the Value of Suffering: An Aw(e)ful Rowing Toward God.* Collegeville, MN: Liturgical Press, 1998.

República Peruana. "Comisión Especial del Senado sobre las Causas de la Violencia y Alternativas de Pacificación en el Perú." In *Violencia y Pacificación.* Lima: DESCO y la Comisión Andina de Juristas, 1989.

Rivera Gónzales, Isabel. *Síntesis de la experiencia de acompañamiento en las comunidades cristianas por agentes pastorals.* Lima: Parroquia La Virgen de Nazaret, 1996.

Rolfes, mcs, Hanni. "Nueva Evangelización." In *La Nueva Evangelización: reflexiones, experiencias y testimonios desde el Perú,* ed. Francisco Rejón Moreno. Lima: Instituto Bartolomé de Las Casas-Rímac, 1992.

Rosada Nunes, María José F. (sic). "Women's Voices in Latin American Theology." *Concilium* 1 (1996): 5.

Rudolph, James D. *Peru: The Evolution of a Crisis.* Westport, CT: Praeger Publishers, 1992.

Ruether, Rosemary Radford. *Liberation Theology: Human Hope Confronts Christian History and American Power.* New York: Paulist Press, 1972.

Sassen, Saskia. *Globalization and Its Discontents.* New York: New Press, 1998.

Say, Elizabeth. *Evidence on Her Own Behalf: Women's Narrative as Theological Voice.* Savage, MD: Rowman & Littlefield, 1990.

Schreiter, Robert J. *The New Catholicity: Theology between the Global and the Local.* Maryknoll, NY: Orbis Books, 1997.

Schüssler Fiorenza, Elisabeth, ed. *The Power of Naming: A Concilium Reader in Feminist Liberation Theology.* Maryknoll, NY: Orbis Books, 1996.

Segundo, Juan Luis. "The Shift Within Latin American Theology." *Journal of Theology for Southern Africa* 52 (1985): 22.

Silverblatt, Irene. "Moon, Sun, Witches." In *The Peru Reader: History, Culture, Politics*, eds. Orin Starn, Carlos Iván Degregori, and Robin Kirk, 35–48. Durham, NC: Duke University Press, 1995.

Smith, Michael L. "Shining Path's Urban Strategy: Ate Vitarte." In *The Shining Path of Peru*, ed. David Scott Palmer. New York: St. Martin's, 1992.

Society of Jesus. *Documents of the Thirty-fourth General Congregation of the Society of Jesus*. St. Louis: Institute of Jesuit Sources, 1995.

Tamez, Elsa, ed. *Against Machismo: Ruben Alves, Leonardo Boff, Gustavo Gutiérrez, José Miguez Bonino, Juan Luis Segundo and Others Talk about the Struggle of Women*. Oak Park, IL: Meyer-Stone Books, 1987.

———, ed. *Las Mujeres Toman la Palabra*. San José, Costa Rica: Editorial Departamento Ecunémico de Investigaciones, 1989.

Tanner, Kathryn. *Theories of Culture: A New Agenda for Theology*. Minneapolis: Fortress Press, 1997.

Tax, Meredith et al. *El Poder de la Palabra: Cultura, Censura y Voz*. Lima: Ediciones Flora Tristan, 1996.

Thurston, Anne. *Because of Her Testimony: The Word in Female Experience*. New York: Crossroad Publishing, 1995.

Tracy, David. *On Naming the Present: Reflections on God, Hermeneutics, and Church*. Maryknoll, NY: Orbis Books, 1994.

Tristan, Flora. *The Worker's Union*. Chicago: University of Illinois Press, 1983.

Tulchin, Joseph S. and Gary Bland, eds. *Peru in Crisis: Dictatorship or Democracy?* Boulder, CO: Lynne Rienner Publishers, 1994.

United Nations Development Programme. *Domestic Violence in Peru*. New York: United Nations, 1999.

U.S. Department of State. Background Notes: Peru. Bureau of Western Hemisphere Affairs. U.S. Department of State Website: *www.state.gov/www.background_notes/*, August 1999.

Valdes Echenique, Teresa and Enrique Gonzalez Moraga, eds. *Mujeres Latinoamericanas en Cifras*. Santiago: Facultad Latinoamericana de Ciencias Sociales, 1993.

Vance-Trembath, Sally M. "John Paul II's *Ut unum sint* and Conversation with Women." *Theological Studies* 60:1 (March 1999): 107–108.

Vega-Centeno B., Imelda. *Aprismo Popular: Cultura, Religión y Política*. Lima: CISEPA, 1991.

Villavicencio, Maritza. *Del Silencio a la Palabra*. Lima: Centro de la Mujer Peruana Flora Tristan, 1992.

Index